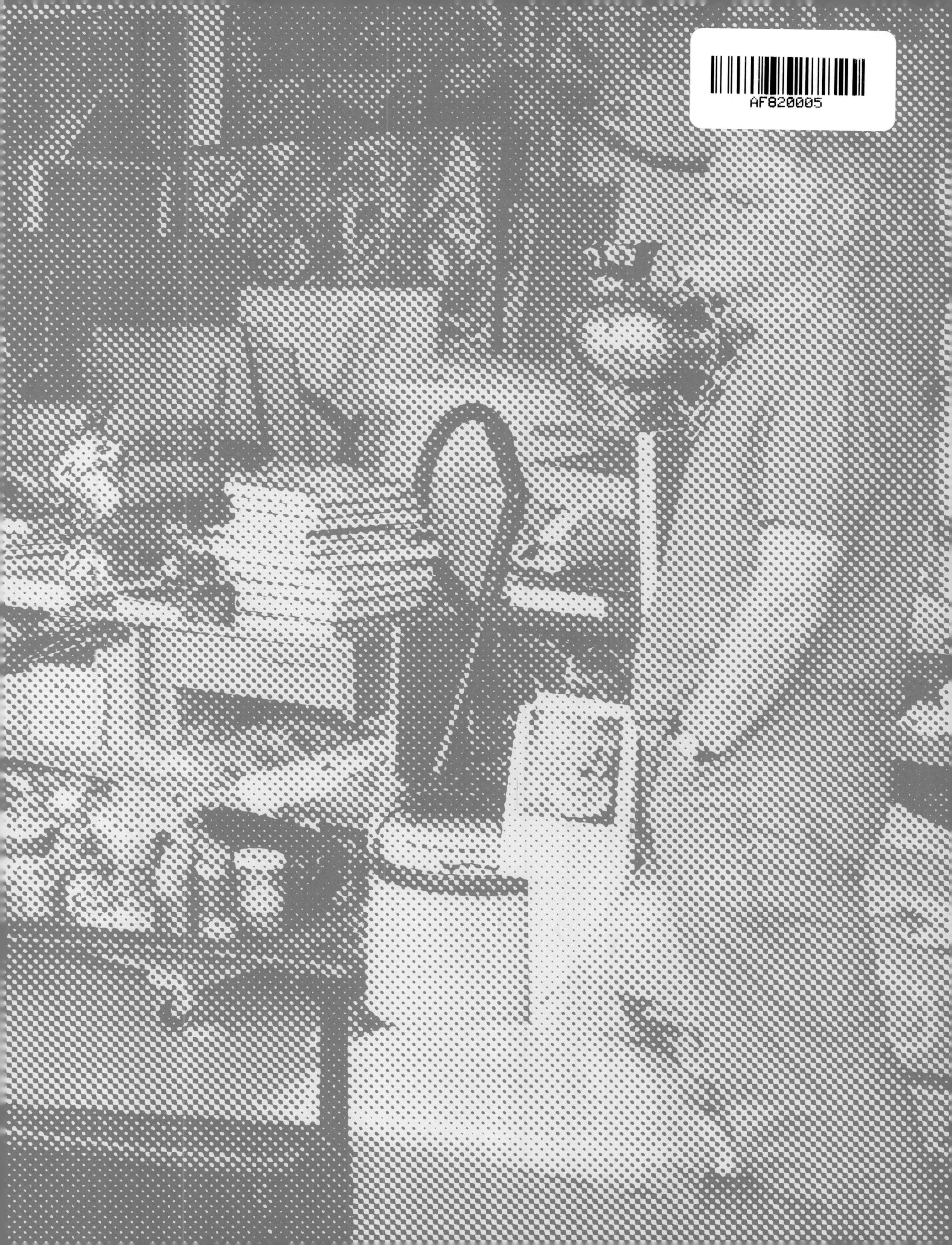

Franz Hitzler

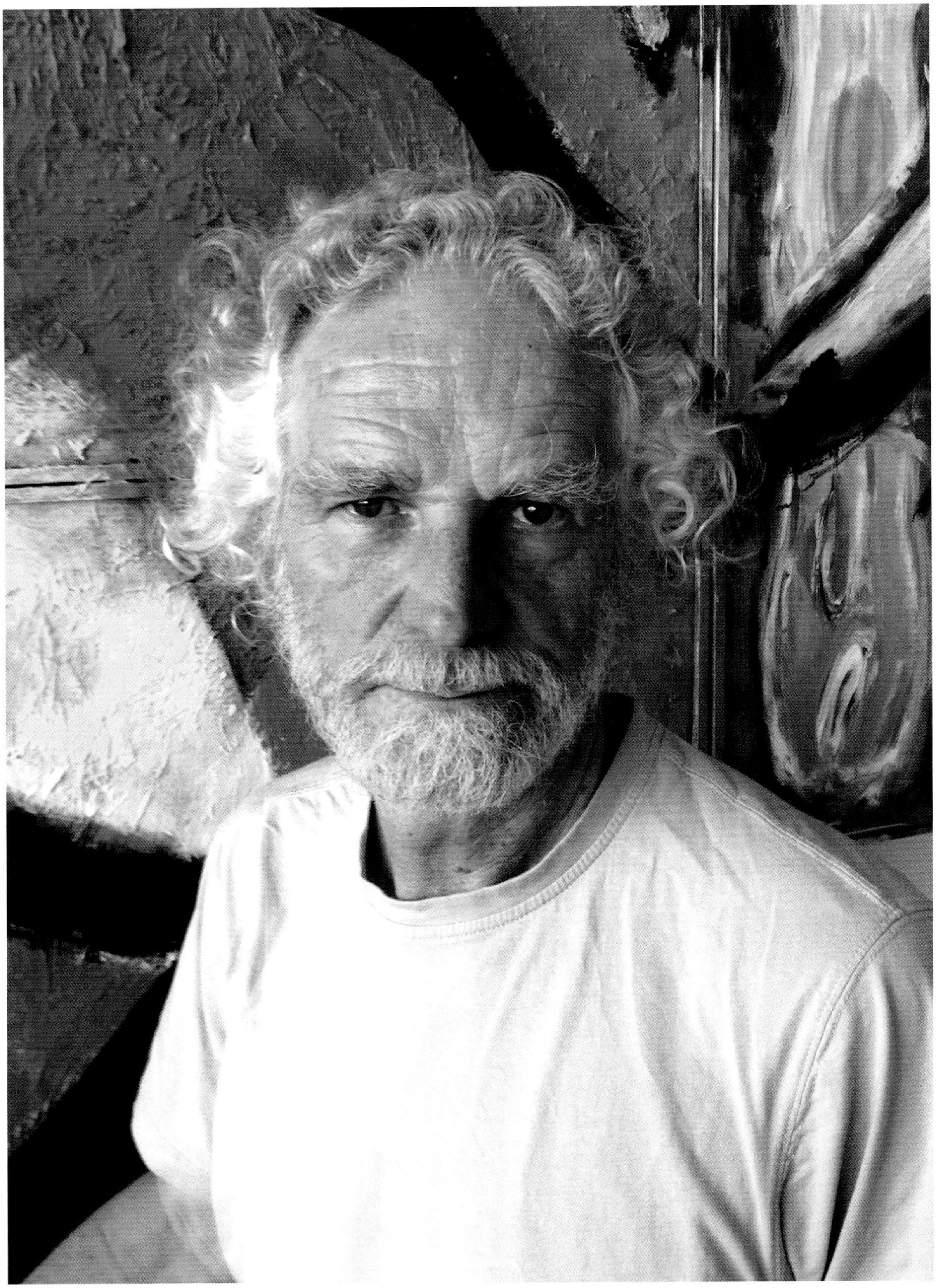

Franz Hitzler

Colour is my Life
Farbe ist mein Leben

Introduction by
Einführung von

Wolfgang Jean Stock

Edition Jürgen B. Tesch

Prestel

Munich · London · New York

Acknowledgements

I should like to express my grateful thanks to those collectors of my works over the past years whose financial support has made the publication of this book possible, especially HRH Franz, Duke of Bavaria, Kurt Schäfer, Bernhard Schaub, Anton and Kati Schick and Helga Schäfer.

My thanks are also due to gallery owners Peter Femfert of DIE GALERIE, Frankfurt, and Otto van de Loo and Marie-José van de Loo in Munich.

The high-quality reproductions of my pictures would not have been possible without the excellent work of the photographers Richard Beer, Munich; Peter Leutsch, Schwebheim; Jens Mauritz, Munich; Elke Mohr, Frankfurt and Toni Ott, Landshut. I am grateful to them for their support.

This book focuses predominantly on more recent works produced during the past ten years, and so many faithful friends who accompanied and supported me during my earlier years are not mentioned by name.

I am very grateful to them all, especially my long-standing first gallery owner, Fred Jahn, who enabled me to embark on life as an independent artist. I should like to thank my publisher, Jürgen B. Tesch, upon whose initiative this publication has been produced, for accompanying the work throughout production together with the book designer Rainer Lienemann.

I am grateful to Wolfgang Jean Stock for his insightful introduction.

I could not have achieved all this without the support of my wife, Katharina Ponnier, who continues to accompany me through the ups and downs of everyday life. To her especially I offer my heartfelt thanks.

October 2012 Franz Hitzler

Dank

Für die finanzielle Unterstützung zu der Herausgabe dieses Buches danke ich meinen langjährigen Sammlern, insbesondere S. K. H. Herzog Franz von Bayern, sowie Kurt Schäfer, Bernhard Schaub, Anton und Kati Schick und Helga Schäfer.

Ferner den Galeristen Peter Femfert, DIE GALERIE, Frankfurt, sowie Otto van de Loo und Marie-José van de Loo, München.

Für die guten Reproduktionen meiner Bilder war die hervorragende Arbeit der Fotografen Richard Beer, München; Peter Leutsch, Schwebheim; Jens Mauritz, München; Elke Mohr, Frankfurt und Toni Ott, Landshut, Voraussetzung. Ihnen gilt mein besonderer Dank für ihre Unterstützung.

Dieses Buch zeigt überwiegend neuere Arbeiten aus den letzten zehn Jahren, und somit sind viele Getreue, die mich in den frühen Jahren begleitet und unterstützt haben, nicht genannt. Ihnen allen bin ich zu großem Dank verpflichtet, insbesondere auch meinem langjährigen, ersten Galeristen Fred Jahn, der mir den Start in ein unabhängiges Künstlerleben ermöglicht hat. Meinem Verleger Jürgen B. Tesch danke ich für die Initiative zu dieser Publikation und seine Begleitung während der Produktion, gemeinsam mit dem Buchgestalter Rainer Lienemann.

Wolfgang Jean Stock ist für die kenntnisreiche Einführung zu danken.

Ohne die Unterstützung meiner Frau, Katharina Ponnier, die mir in Höhen und Tiefen des Lebens zur Seite steht, hätte ich dies alles nicht realisieren können, ihr gilt mein besonders herzlicher Dank.

Oktober 2012 Franz Hitzler

Projecting One's Entire Existence into the Picture

On the expressive painting of Franz Hitzler

Three decades ago, in the years after 1980, the international art world once again gazed wide-eyed towards Germany. A phenomenon could be observed in the western part of the country, and not least in West Berlin: the appearance of an entire generation of young artists who dedicated themselves with determination to painting, a medium that only a short time previously had been described by influential critics as obsolete. There were art-historical reasons why this type of painting, described as "vigorous" or "defiant", should arouse such a broadly-based response in artists' associations and groups. The concentrated presence of expressive-figurative pictures was seen as the return of a 'typically German' tradition. In Berlin, the young painters took as their subject the nocturnal, often bizarre life of the city, while those in Hamburg or Cologne had no qualms about incorporating jokes or cynicism. But virtually nothing is heard today of many of the artists who were celebrated at that time in exhibitions and publications.

In addition to various artistic groups, however, a number of artists who were clearly solitary individuals also aroused attention at the time. Among them was the Munich-based painter Franz Hitzler, born in 1946. The specific characteristics of his art became particularly evident in the international exhibition *aktuell '83* at the Lenbachhaus in Munich. His pictures were remarkable for their wildness, their impetuous interweaving of figurative elements and free forms, as well as through applications that pointed into the third dimension and at the same time beyond the edge of the picture. Viewers sensed that these pictures were not a reaction to cues from the outer world, but that they were produced as the result of existential feelings of oppression and personal endangerment. The earnest striving to explain one's own existence through artistic means has remained Hitzler's main concern to this day.

Hell on Earth

Drawing conclusions about artists' lives from their work is often rather a questionable approach. In the case of Hitzler, however, childhood and youth form the foundations on which his painting has developed. Although he grew up in an artistically inclined family and was trained as a singer (his father is a church organist and teacher), the course of his early years was a dramatic one. Hitzler was constantly taken to task by his father as well as by his teacher and the local priest, becoming their "whipping boy". On the one hand, he experienced a religious dimension through his singing – and on the other, his everyday life was made hell. This conflict led to an inner loneliness: "All I really had left, the

Die ganze Existenz ins Bild werfen

Zur expressiven Malerei von Franz Hitzler

Vor drei Jahrzehnten, in den Jahren nach 1980, schaute die internationale Kunstwelt wieder einmal mit großen Augen nach Deutschland. In dessen westlichem Teil, nicht zuletzt in West-Berlin, war ein Phänomen zu bestaunen – der Auftritt einer ganzen Generation junger Künstler, die sich mit Vehemenz der Malerei widmeten, einem Medium, das kurz zuvor noch von einflussreichen Kritikern als überholt bezeichnet worden war. Dass diese als „heftig" oder „frech" charakterisierte Malerei von Künstlergruppen und Gruppierungen eine derart breite Resonanz finden konnte, hatte auch kunstgeschichtliche Gründe: Das geballte Auftreten expressiv-figurativer Bilder wurde als Wiederkehr einer ‚typisch deutschen' Tradition verstanden. In Berlin machten die jungen Maler das nächtliche, oft bizarre Großstadtleben zum Thema, in Hamburg oder in Köln schreckten sie auch nicht vor Ulk oder Zynismus zurück. Doch von etlichen jener Künstler, die damals in Ausstellungen und Publikationen gefeiert wurden, ist heute kaum mehr die Rede.
Neben diversen Künstlergruppen sorgten seinerzeit aber auch offensichtliche Einzelgänger für Aufmerksamkeit. Zu ihnen gehörte der 1946 geborene Münchner Maler Franz Hitzler. Die Eigenarten seiner Kunst wurden dann bei der internationalen Ausstellung *aktuell '83* im Münchner Lenbachhaus besonders deutlich. Seine Bilder fielen auf durch ihre Wildheit, durch eine ungestüme Verschränkung von figurativen Elementen und freien Formen, aber auch durch Applikationen, welche in die dritte Dimension und zugleich über den Bildrand hinauswiesen. Man spürte, dass diese Bilder nicht auf Anlässe der Außenwelt reagierten, sondern aus existenzieller Beklemmung und persönlicher Gefährdung entstanden waren. Das ernsthafte Bestreben, die eigene Existenz mit künstlerischen Mitteln zu klären, ist bis heute Hitzlers großes Thema geblieben.

Hölle auf Erden

Es ist bei Künstlern oft etwas fragwürdig, vom Leben auf das Werk zu schließen. Bei Hitzler jedoch bilden Kindheit und Jugend den Wurzelgrund seiner Malerei. Obwohl er in einer musischen Familie aufwächst (der Vater ist Kirchenmusiker und Lehrer) und eine Gesangsausbildung erhält, verlaufen seine frühen Jahre dramatisch. Sowohl vom Vater als auch vom Pfarrer und vom Lehrer wird Hitzler als „Prügelknabe" ständig gezüchtigt. Auf der einen Seite erfährt er beim Singen eine religiöse Dimension – auf der anderen Seite wird ihm der Alltag zur Hölle gemacht. Dieser Zwiespalt führt in eine innerliche Einsamkeit: „Das Einzige, was eigentlich blieb, was mich gerettet hat, war

only thing that saved me, was nature, apart from painting and drawing. Most of my social relationships were destroyed. So I decided that I would leave that environment." At the age of fifteen, Hitzler made his way to Amsterdam in order to see the works of Rembrandt, which had deeply moved him even as reproductions in books. "There was a dimension of light in his paintings that had something to do with the space I had experienced as a choirboy. And at the same time, the tremendous dimension of suffering that is expressed in his late self-portraits." The attempt to save himself through Rembrandt was successful. In the following year, 1962, Hitzler began to study painting, initially at the College of Art in Augsburg, and then later at the Academy of Fine Arts in Munich, where he became a master student of Franz Nagel.

Liberation from the life crisis

Until the early 1970s, Hitzler was able to dissociate himself from the traumatic experiences of his childhood. But then he found himself in a life crisis that drove him to the very extremes of his existence, even physically. He saved himself a second time: instead of continuing to suppress the humiliations he had suffered, he made them a subject of his work. He created his "Schreckensbilder" (Visions of Terror), filled with ghostlike figures and faces distorted with suffering, which scream out their mental misery in dismal colours. The agonised study of his past led Hitzler towards his own liberation: "I was full of enthusiasm and strength when I painted these visions of terror." A few years later, after 1980, a break occurred whose effects can still be felt to this day. Dissatisfied with traditional panel painting, whose "beauty" he felt was not sufficiently realistic, Hitzler began processing his pictures in a massive way: he slit the surfaces or folded them outwards; he laced them together or added appliqué sections. By processing and assembling his pictures in this way, Hitzler gave them multiple planes that were full of tension and transformed them into three-dimensional objects.

Vitality as a benchmark

Of course, the use of non-painterly means should attract the viewer's attention not only through formal means. When Hitzler says that each time he projects his entire existence into the picture, it is for him above all a question of remaining true to himself. Vitality is the key concept in his painting: "Man gains vitality when he succeeds in integrating all aspects of his innermost being into his life, not only the most dreadful experiences, but also the dimension of his utmost longings. This means that there is an internal exchange between these two moments within his reality that at first sight appear to be total extremes. This exchange is in fact the vitality I refer to. I need not give up anything of myself, but succeed in integrating everything, in other words, also the fear of myself, my actual reality. That must be taken up into a spiritualised, redemptive or disengaging dimension in the process of transformation." Hitzler is thus

die Natur, und dann das Malen und Zeichnen. Die meisten sozialen Beziehungen waren vernichtet. Da habe ich beschlossen, dieses Umfeld einfach zu verlassen.“ Im Alter von fünfzehn Jahren schlägt sich Hitzler nach Amsterdam durch, um dort Werke von Rembrandt zu sehen, die ihn schon als Abbildungen in Büchern tief berührt haben: „Da war eine Lichtdimension in dieser Malerei, die mit dem Raum zu tun hatte, den ich als Sängerknabe erlebt hatte. Zugleich diese große Leiderfahrung, die in seinen späten Selbstbildnissen zum Ausdruck kommt.“ Der Rettungsversuch mit Rembrandt gelingt. Im Jahr darauf, 1962, nimmt Hitzler das Studium der Malerei auf, zunächst an der Werkkunstschule in Augsburg, dann an der Kunstakademie in München, wo er Meisterschüler von Franz Nagel wird.

Befreiung aus der Lebenskrise

Bis in die frühen siebziger Jahre hinein kann Hitzler die traumatischen Erlebnisse seiner Kindheit abspalten. Doch dann erfasst ihn eine Lebenskrise, die ihn auch körperlich an den Rand seiner Existenz bringt. Da rettet er sich ein zweites Mal: Statt die erlittenen Demütigungen weiter zu verdrängen, macht er sie zum Thema. Es entstehen seine „Schreckensbilder“ mit gespensterhaften Gestalten und vom Leid verzerrten Gesichtern, die das seelische Elend in düsteren Farben herausschreien. Die qualvolle Auseinandersetzung mit der Vergangenheit führt Hitzler auf den Weg der Befreiung: „Ich hatte große Begeisterung und Kraft, als ich diese Schreckensbilder gemalt habe.“ Wenige Jahre später, nach 1980, kommt es zu einer großen, bis heute nachwirkenden Zäsur. Unzufrieden mit der traditionellen Tafelmalerei, deren „Schönheit“ er für sich als zu wenig wahrhaftig empfindet, beginnt Hitzler seine Bilder massiv zu bearbeiten: Er schlitzt die Flächen auf oder klappt sie nach außen, er setzt Verschnürungen ein oder bringt Applikationen an. Durch diese Eingriffe und Montagen erhalten die Bilder nicht nur mehrere spannungsreiche Ebenen, sondern werden auch zu räumlichen Objekten.

Lebendigkeit als Maßstab

Die Verwendung nicht-malerischer Mittel soll freilich nicht nur formal faszinieren. Wenn Hitzler sagt, dass er stets aufs Neue seine ganze Existenz ins Bild werfe, so kommt es ihm vor allem darauf an, authentisch zu bleiben. Für seine Malerei ist Lebendigkeit der Schlüsselbegriff: „Der Mensch wird lebendig, wenn er alle Bereiche seiner Innerlichkeit in sein Leben integrieren kann, sowohl die schrecklichsten Erfahrungen als auch seine höchste Sehnsuchtsdimension. Das heißt, dass es einen inneren Austausch gibt zwischen diesen beiden zunächst extremen Momenten seiner Wirklichkeit. Dieser Austausch ist eigentlich schon die Lebendigkeit – wenn ich nichts von mir abspalten muss, sondern alles integrieren kann, also auch das Erschrecken vor mir selbst, meiner tatsächlichen Wirklichkeit. Das muss ja mit aufgenommen werden in den Transformationsprozess, in eine durchgeistigte, lichtere, erlösende oder

both a romantic and a realist. He is a romantic because a deep longing for spiritualisation leads him through his art, a striving for the fulfilment of oneness with the world; and at the same time, he is a realist because he rejects an escape into pure abstraction. Hitzler does not succumb to visions; he examines the contradictions of reality. It is his aim that his pictures should touch all the senses. Each existence is damaged – which is why the artist expects of his works that they endure "injuries". Each individual is capable of many fantasies, which is why Hitzler foregoes neither figurative nor abstract means.

Transcendence through colour

The pictures shown in this book, especially those produced during recent decades, also include works that were overpainted over a long period. For Hitzler, this open process is a part of vitality. He reworked pictures when his own "clarifications" required it. And so we can conclude that the artist was in a different mental state when an originally protean representation subsequently gave way to a calmer structure. From the "abyss" in suffering and pain, from the "fear of the soul" to transcendence: colour is the medium to express this. Hitzler's more recent pictures frequently surprise us with their harmonious, almost serene colour resonances. Colour, for him, has always represented the highest phenomenon of the spirit in our reality: "This means that when a person can make a colour that he perceives resonate perfectly in his innermost being, then he has transformed this area of colour into a reality within himself."

Franz Hitzler is one of the most unconventional German artists of his generation because he combines vitality and erudition, self-critical reflection and a desire for expression in a most unusual manner. His approach corresponds with the attitude of the great cultural sociologist Georg Simmel, in whose publication *Lebensanschauung* from 1918 we can read that to live means to transcend. Hitzler presents us with a heightened, spiritual world. Much to his delight, the encounter is quite different each time: "Each viewer sees his or her own picture."

Wolfgang Jean Stock

The quotations are taken from conversations between the author and Franz Hitzler on 2 December 2010 and 10 September 2012.

lösende Dimension." Hitzler ist somit Romantiker und Realist zugleich. Romantiker, weil ihn eine tiefe Sehnsucht nach Vergeistigung durch Kunst leitet, ein Streben nach erfüllter Einheit mit der Welt, und ebenso Realist, weil er eine Flucht in die reine Abstraktion ablehnt. Hitzler gibt sich nicht Visionen hin, sondern Erkundungen der widersprüchlichen Realität. Seine Bilder sollen alle Sinne berühren. Jede Existenz ist gebrochen – deshalb mutet der Künstler seinen Arbeiten auch „Verwundungen" zu. Der Mensch ist zu vielen Imaginationen fähig. Aus diesem Grund verzichtet Hitzler weder auf figurative noch auf abstrakte Mittel.

Transzendenz durch Farbe

Die in diesem Buch gezeigten, vor allem im letzten Jahrzehnt entstandenen Bilder umfassen auch Arbeiten, die über einen langen Zeitraum hinweg übermalt wurden. Für Hitzler gehört zur Lebendigkeit der offene Prozess. Er hat Bilder dann neu bearbeitet, wenn eigene „Klärungen" danach verlangt haben. So darf man auf eine veränderte Befindlichkeit des Künstlers schließen, wenn eine ursprünglich vielgestaltige Darstellung einem nun ruhigeren Aufbau gewichen ist. Vom „Abgrund" in Leid und Schmerz, vom „Erschrecken der Seele" hin zur Transzendenz: Dafür ist die Farbe das Medium. Hitzlers neuere Bilder überraschen oft durch harmonische, fast heitere Farbklänge. Die Farbe stellt für ihn von jeher das höchste Phänomen des Geistes in unserer Wirklichkeit dar: „Das heißt, wenn der Mensch die Farbe, die er wahrnimmt, in seiner Innerlichkeit vollkommen zum Klingen bringen kann, dann hat er diesen Bereich der Farbe in sich selbst zu einer Realität werden lassen."
Franz Hitzler zählt zu den eigenwilligsten deutschen Künstlern seiner Generation, weil sich in ihm Vitalität und Belesenheit, selbstkritische Reflexion und Ausdrucksverlangen in einer außergewöhnlichen Weise verbinden. In seiner Haltung entspricht er der Auffassung des großen Kultursoziologen Georg Simmel, in dessen Buch *Lebensanschauung* aus dem Jahr 1918 zu lesen ist, Leben bedeute Transzendieren. Hitzler hält uns in seinem Werk eine gesteigerte, eine geistige Welt vor Augen. Die Begegnung mit ihr fällt zu seiner Freude ganz unterschiedlich aus. Denn, so sagt er, „jeder Betrachter sieht sein eigenes Bild".

Wolfgang Jean Stock

Die Zitate entstammen Gesprächen des Autors mit Franz Hitzler am 2. Dezember 2010 und 10 September 2012.

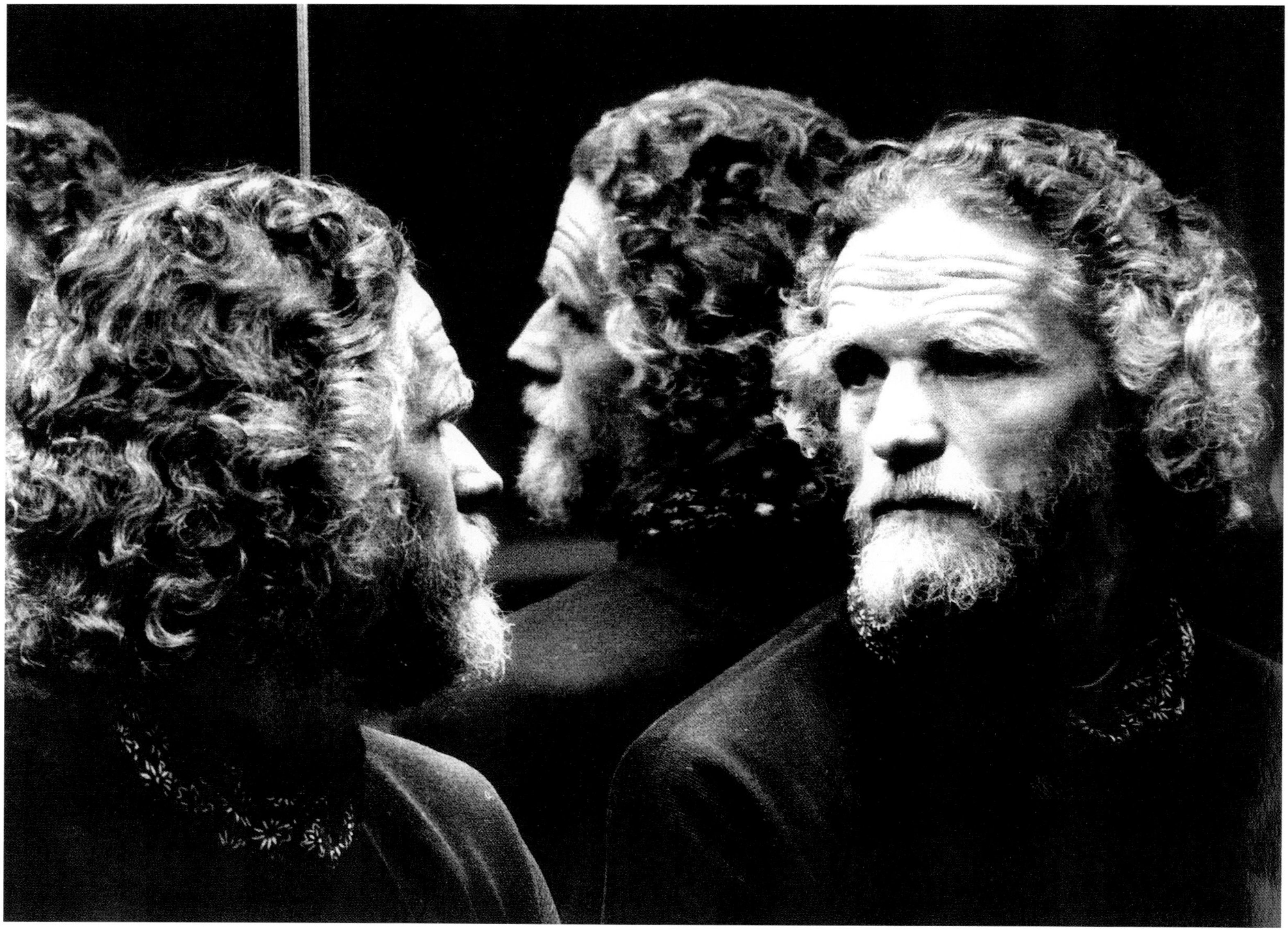

“Painting is the the mischievous game the gods play with my ignorance”

„Malerei ist das närrische Spiel der Gottheit mit meiner Unwissenheit“

Franz Hitzler

Works that have more than one date were either altered or painted over at a later date.

Arbeiten mit mehr als einer Jahreszahl sind zu einem späteren Zeitpunkt ergänzt bzw. übermalt worden.

Dance of Hardship
Tanz der Mühsal

1989/2006
Acrylic on canvas / Acryl auf Leinwand
70 × 55 cm

Otto van de Loo Collection / Sammlung Otto van de Loo

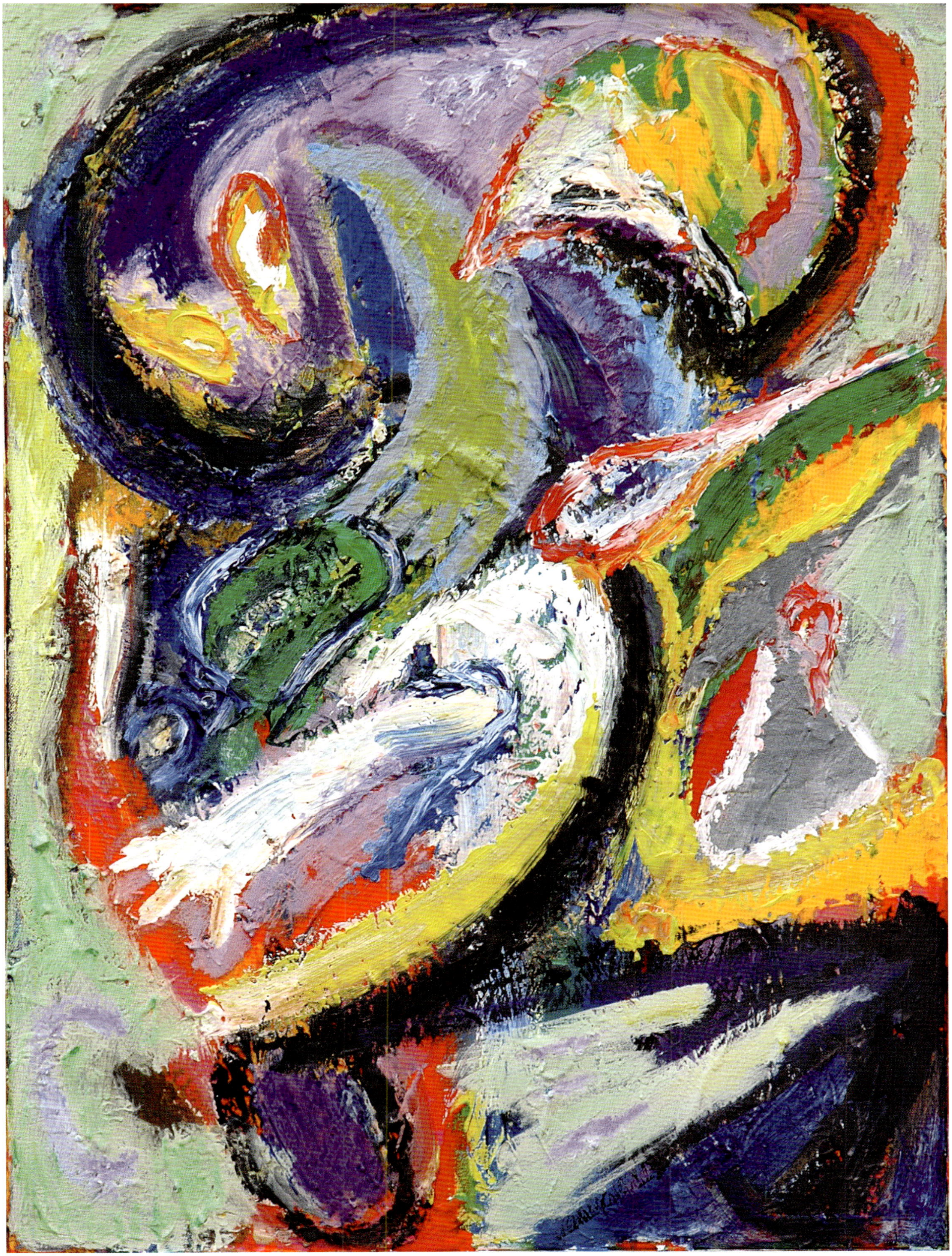

Fire
Brand

2006
Acrylic on canvas / Acryl auf Leinwand
100 × 100 cm

DIE GALERIE, Frankfurt am Main

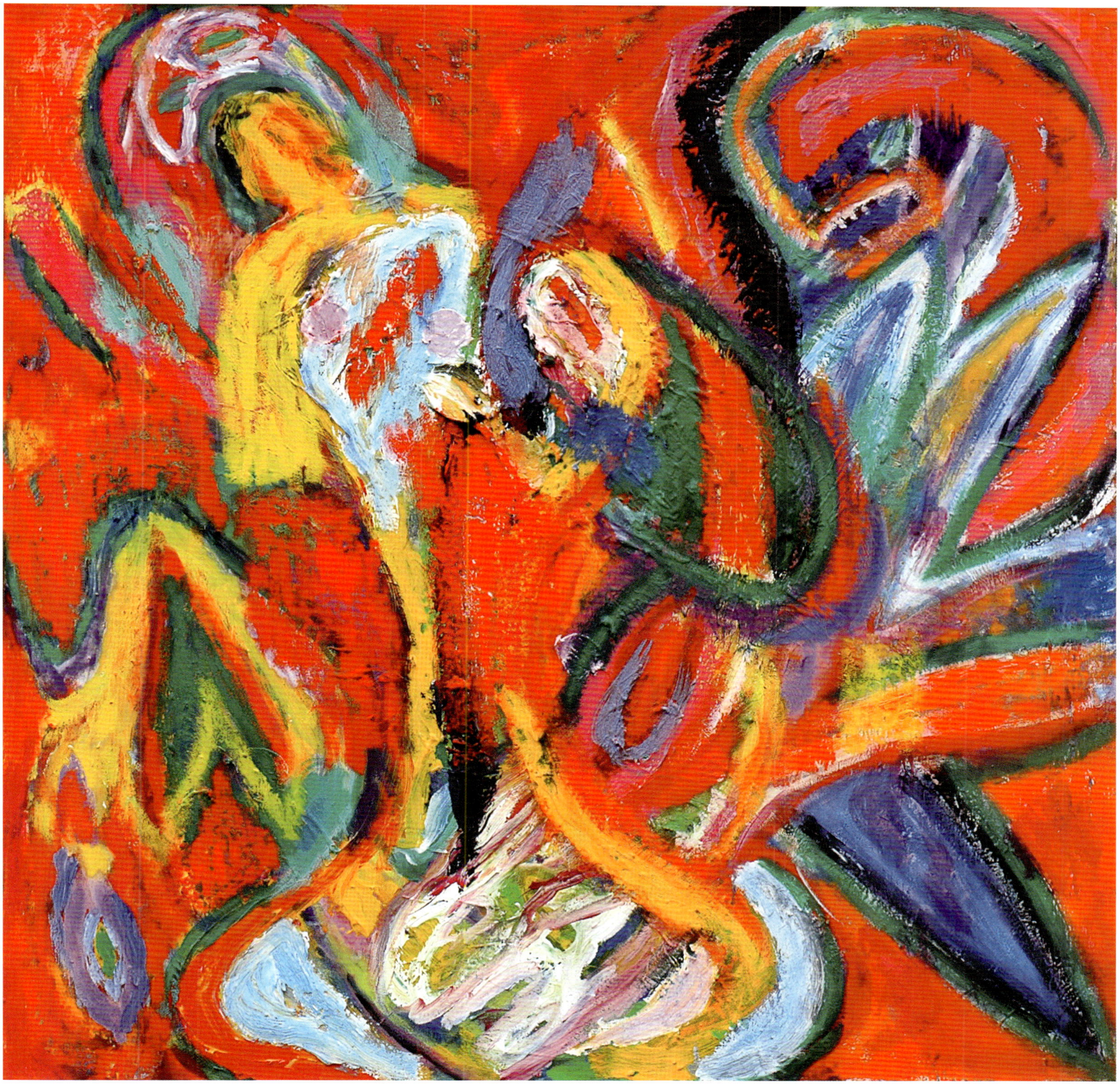

To go through hell you must drive damned well
Wer durch die Hölle will, muss verdammt gut fahren können

2004
Acrylic on canvas / Acryl auf Leinwand
112 × 112 cm

Kurt Schäfer Collection / Sammlung Kurt Schäfer

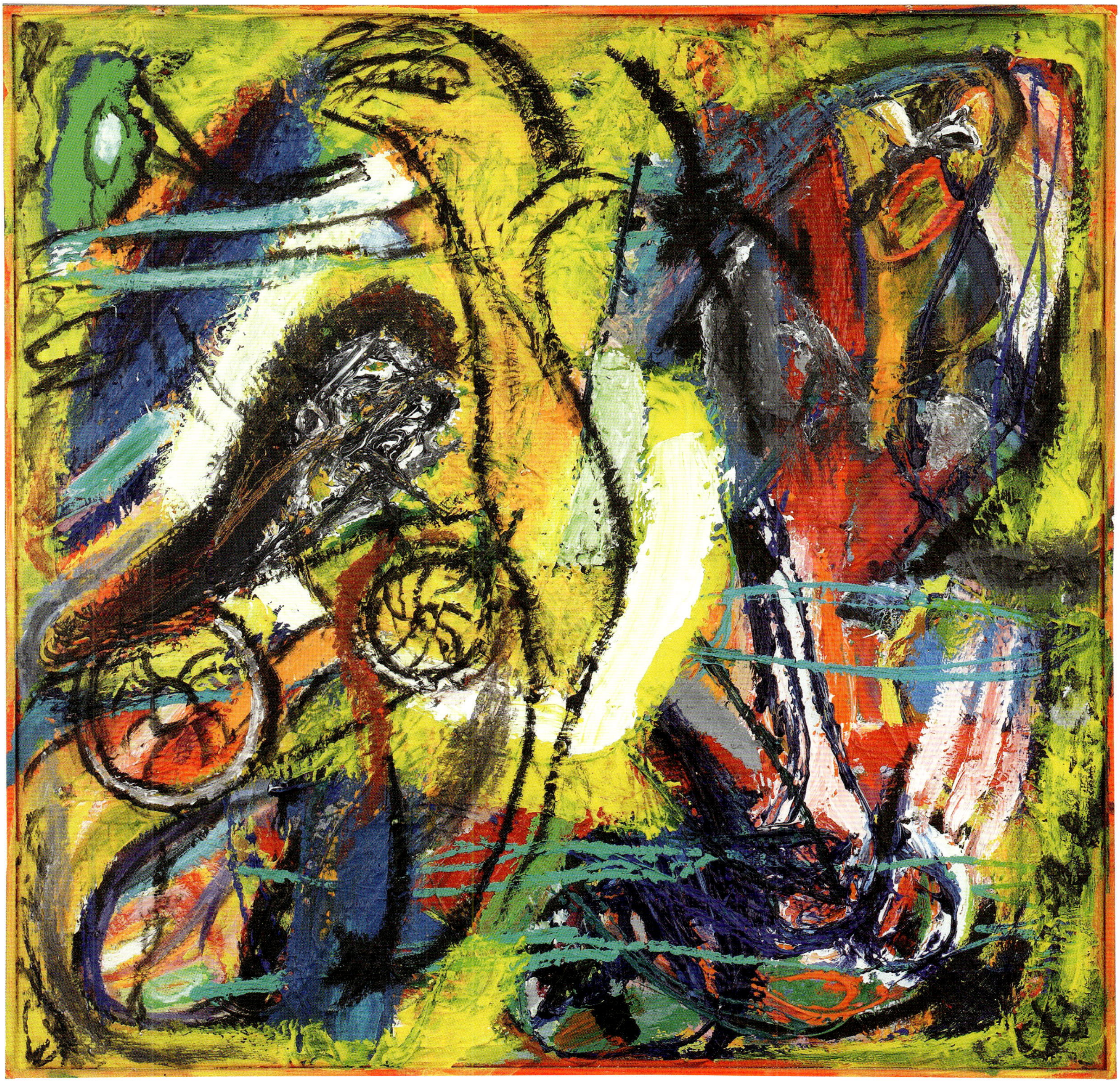

Blue Flame
Blaue Flamme

1993/2000
Acrylic on canvas / Acryl auf Leinwand
152 × 122 cm

HRH Duke Franz of Bavaria Collection / Sammlung SKH Herzog Franz von Bayern

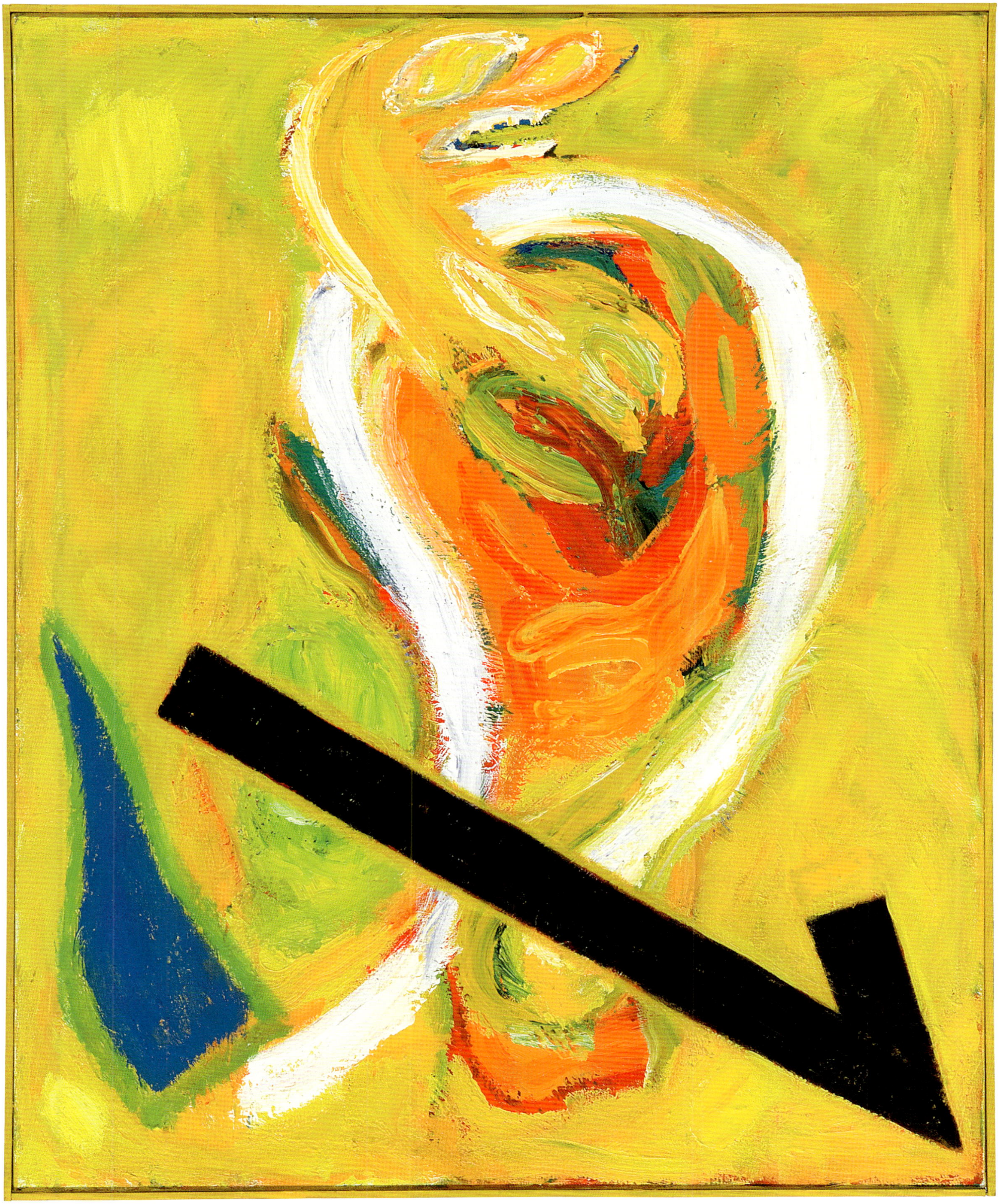

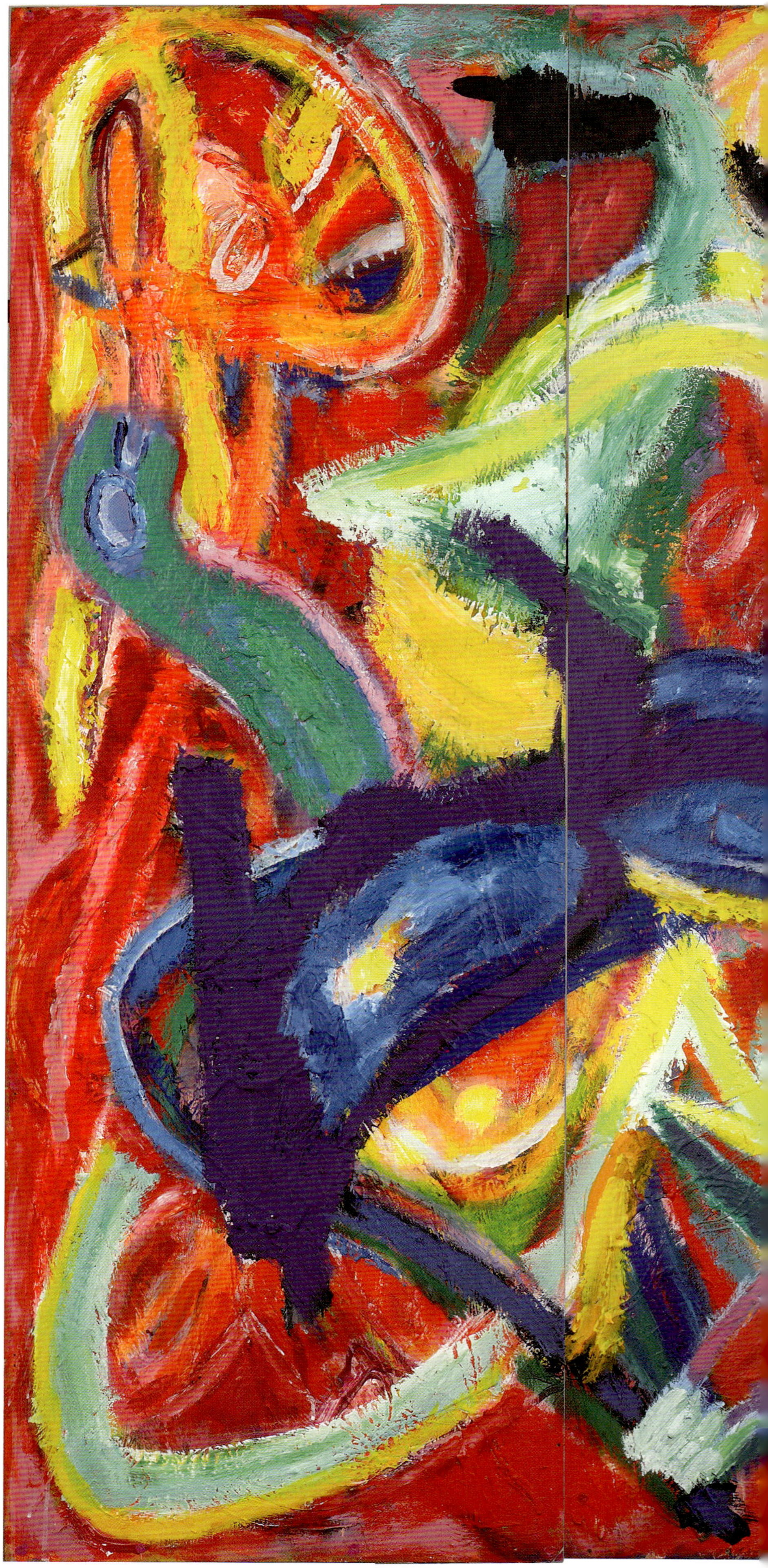

Explosive Blue
Explosives Blau

2007
Acrylic on plywood (3 sections) / Acryl auf Sperrholz (3-teilig)
165 × 228 cm

Kurt Schäfer Collection / Sammlung Kurt Schäfer

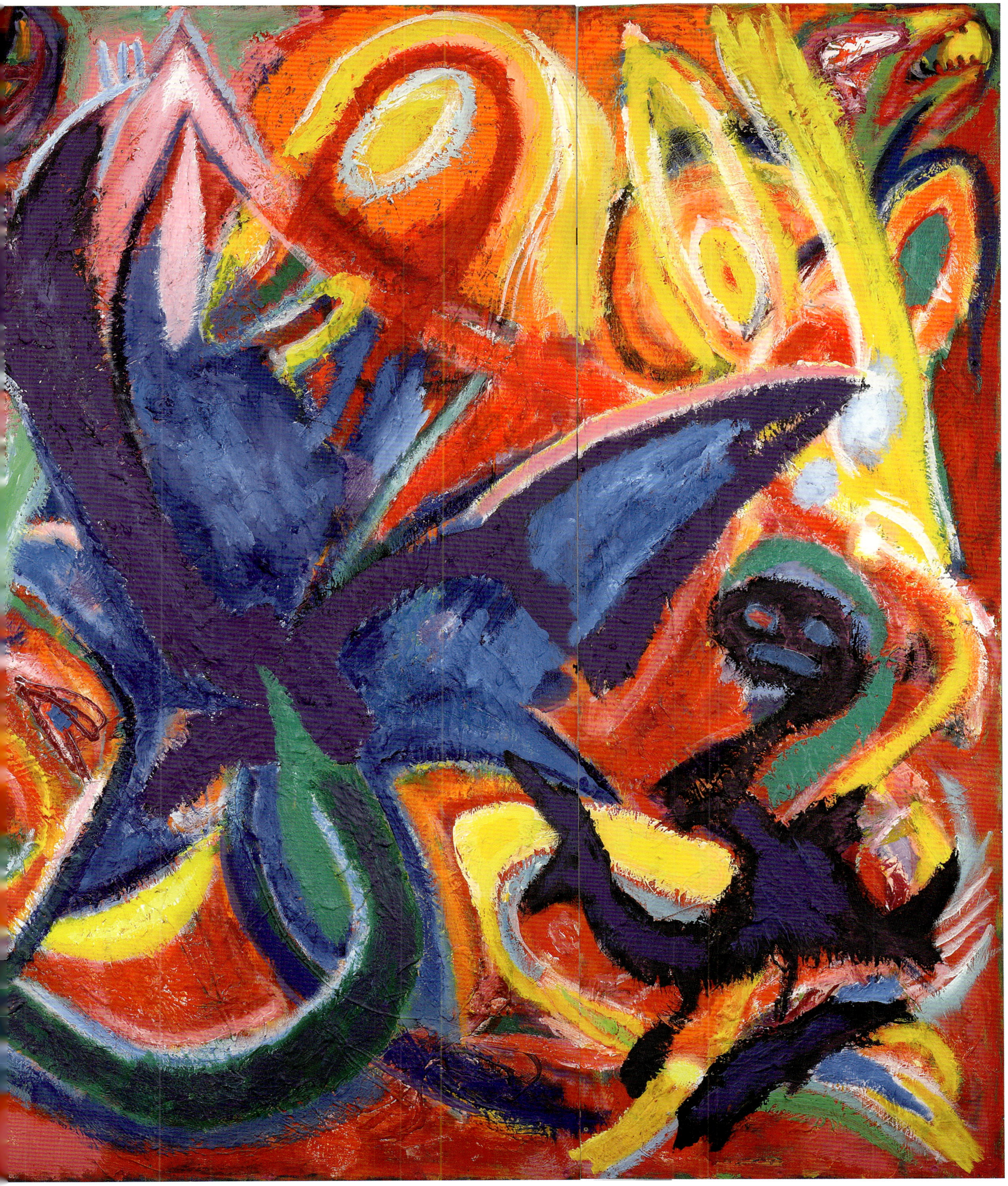

Heart Throb
Herzklopfen

2000
Acrylic on canvas / Acryl auf Leinwand
132 × 102 cm

Private collection, Munich / Privatsammlung München

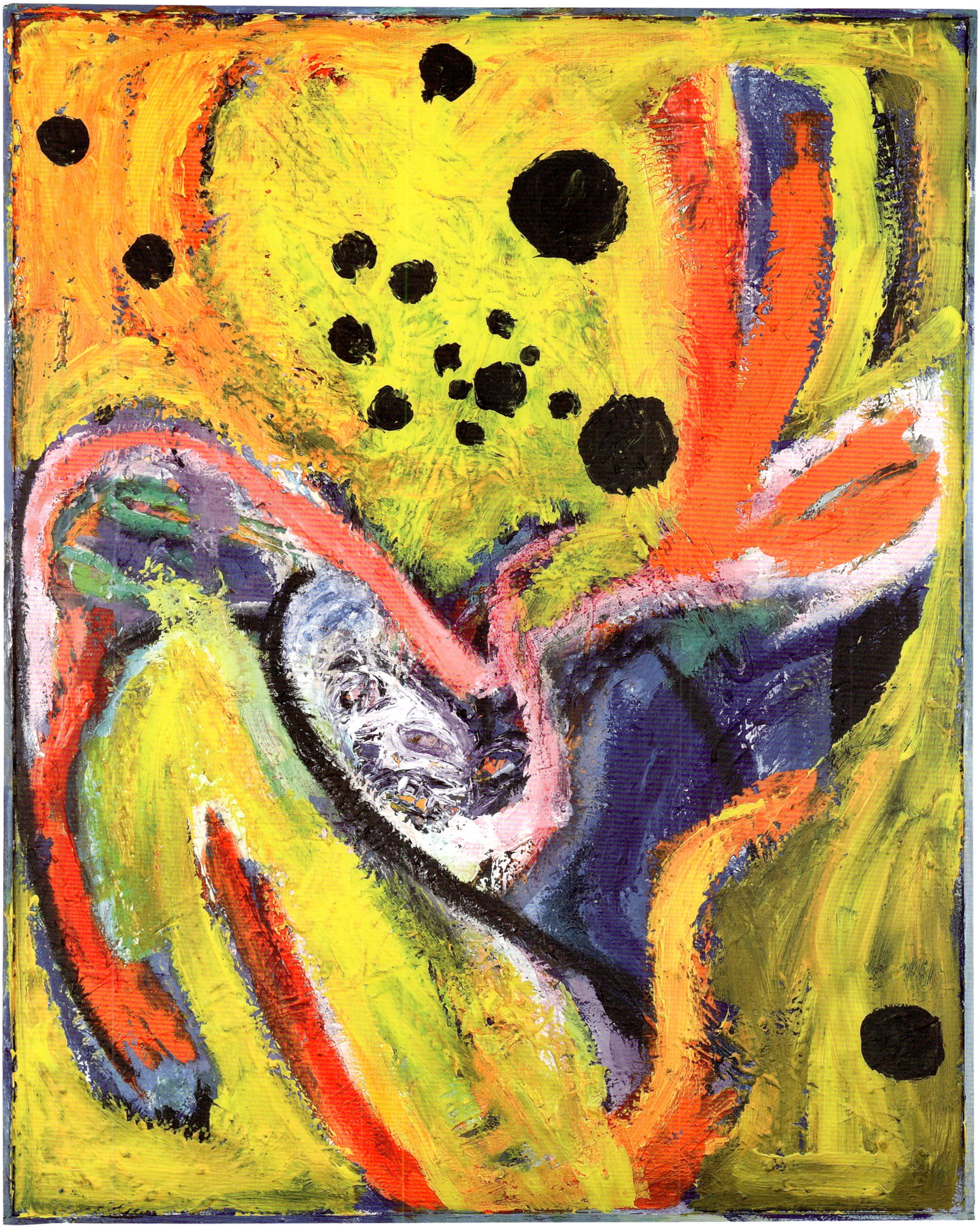

Birth of the Sonata
Geburt der Sonate

2009
Acrylic on canvas / Acryl auf Leinwand
100 × 70 cm

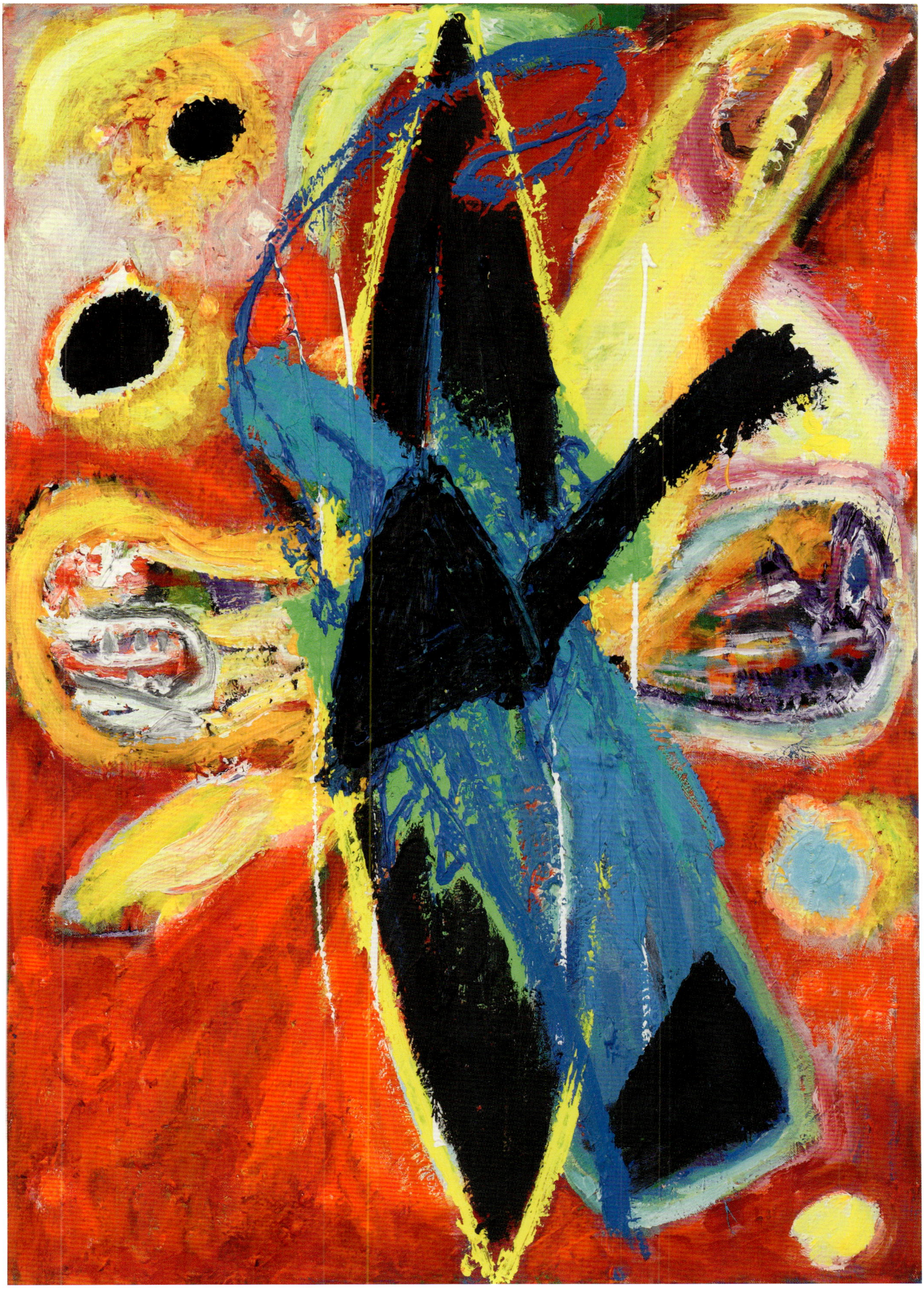

Winged Blue
Blau geflügelt

1990/2011/2012
Acrylic on canvas / Acryl auf Leinwand
112 × 77 cm

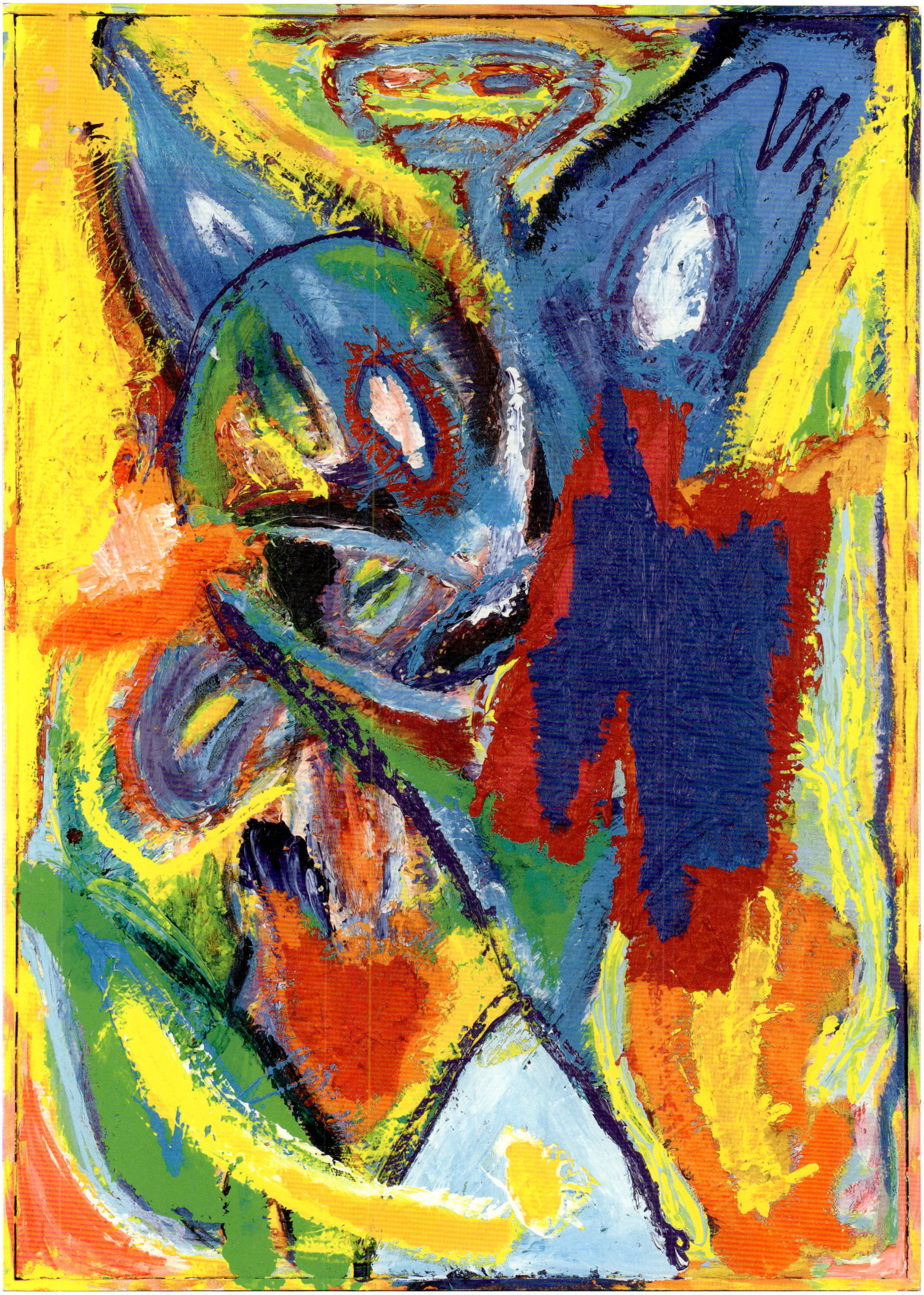

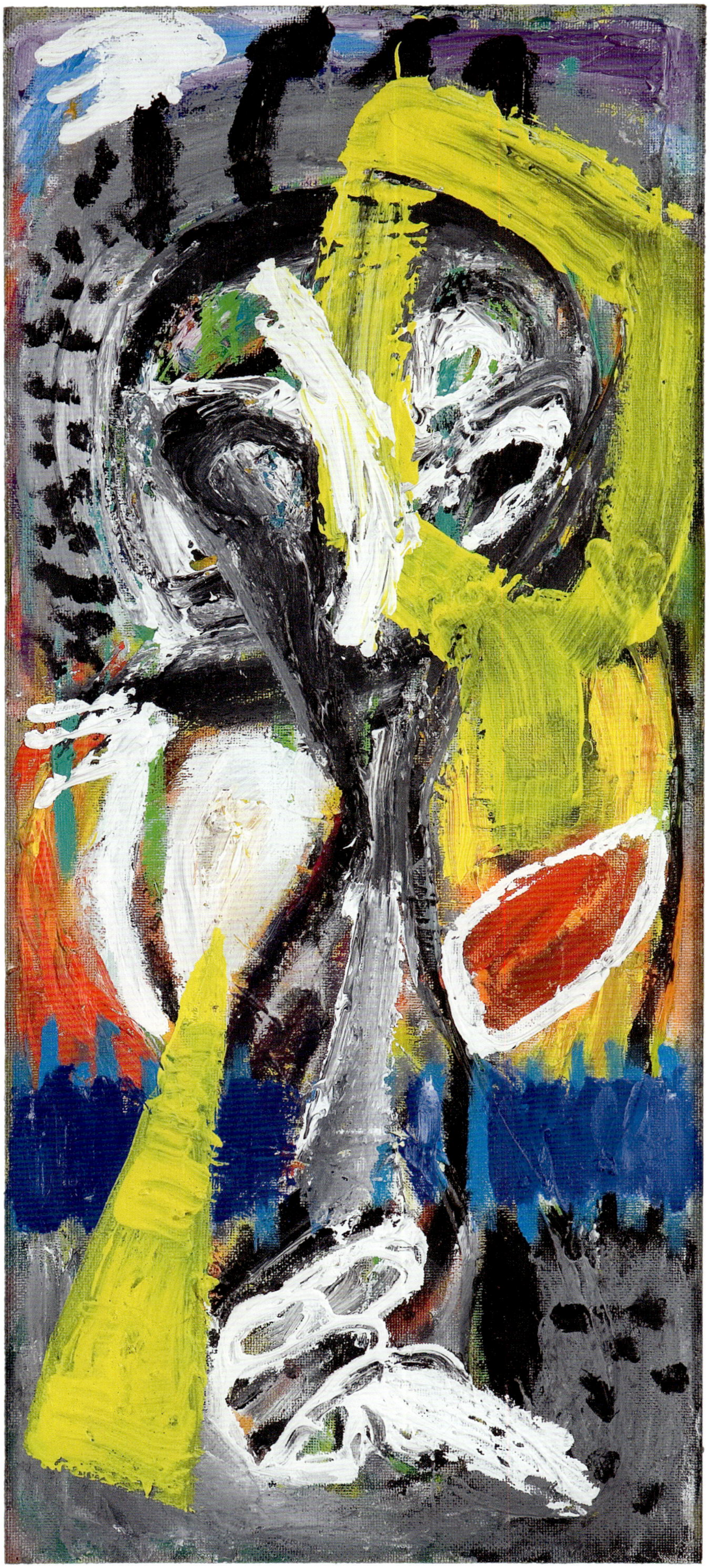

What will he decide on?
Wofür wird er sich entscheiden?

1999/2002/2003
Acrylic on hardboard / Acryl auf Hartfaserplatte
82 × 36 cm

Schick Collection / Sammlung Schick

Message from the Depths
Botschaft aus der Tiefe

2004
Acrylic on canvas/ Acryl auf Leinwand
92 × 72 cm

Schick Collection / Sammlung Schick

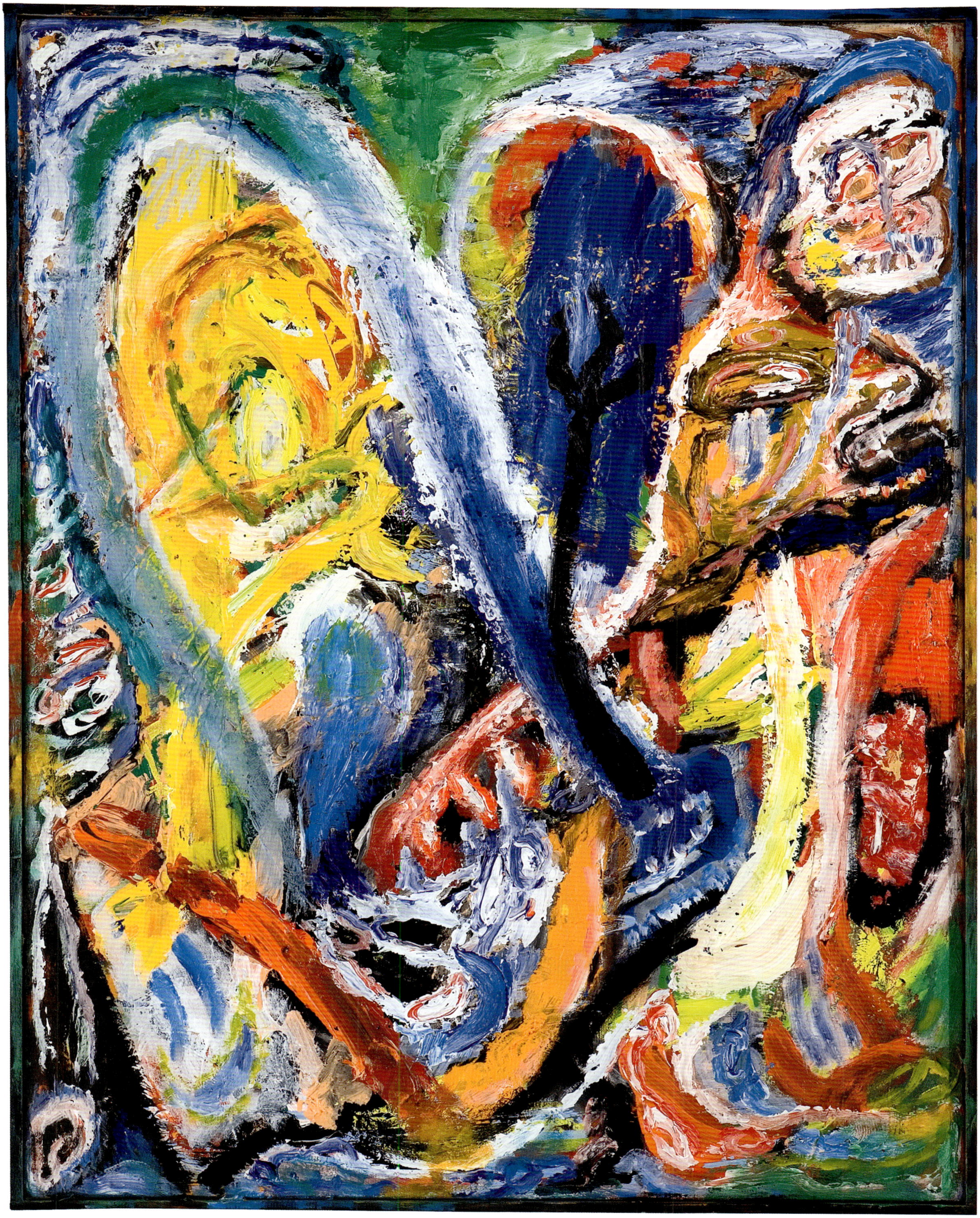

Further Down
Etwas unterhalb

2005
Acrylic on canvas / Acryl auf Leinwand
95 × 60 cm

Galerie van de Loo Projekte

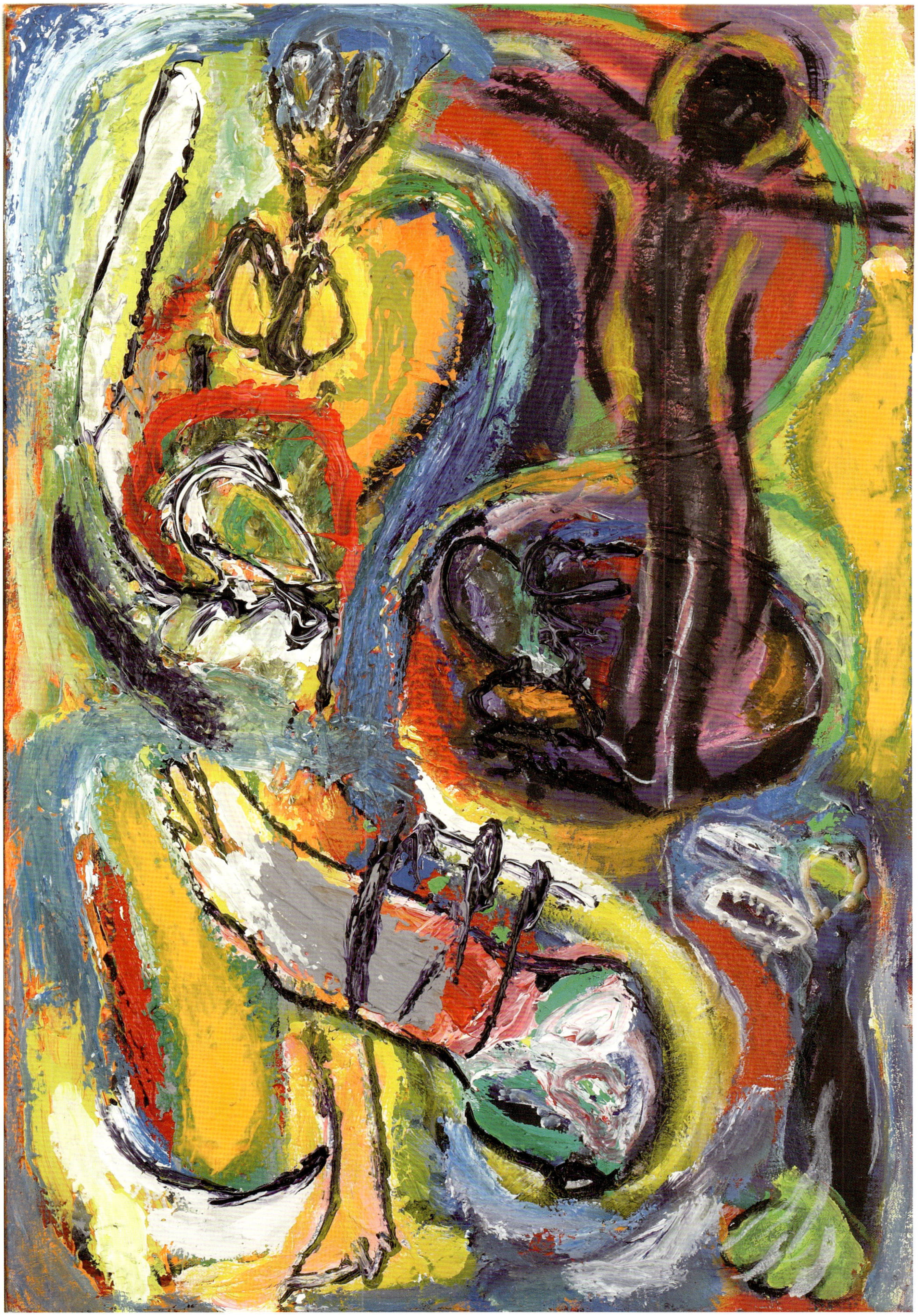

Tears of Anna Magdalena
Tränen von Anna Magdalena

2009
Acrylic on canvas / Acryl auf Leinwand
122 × 82 cm

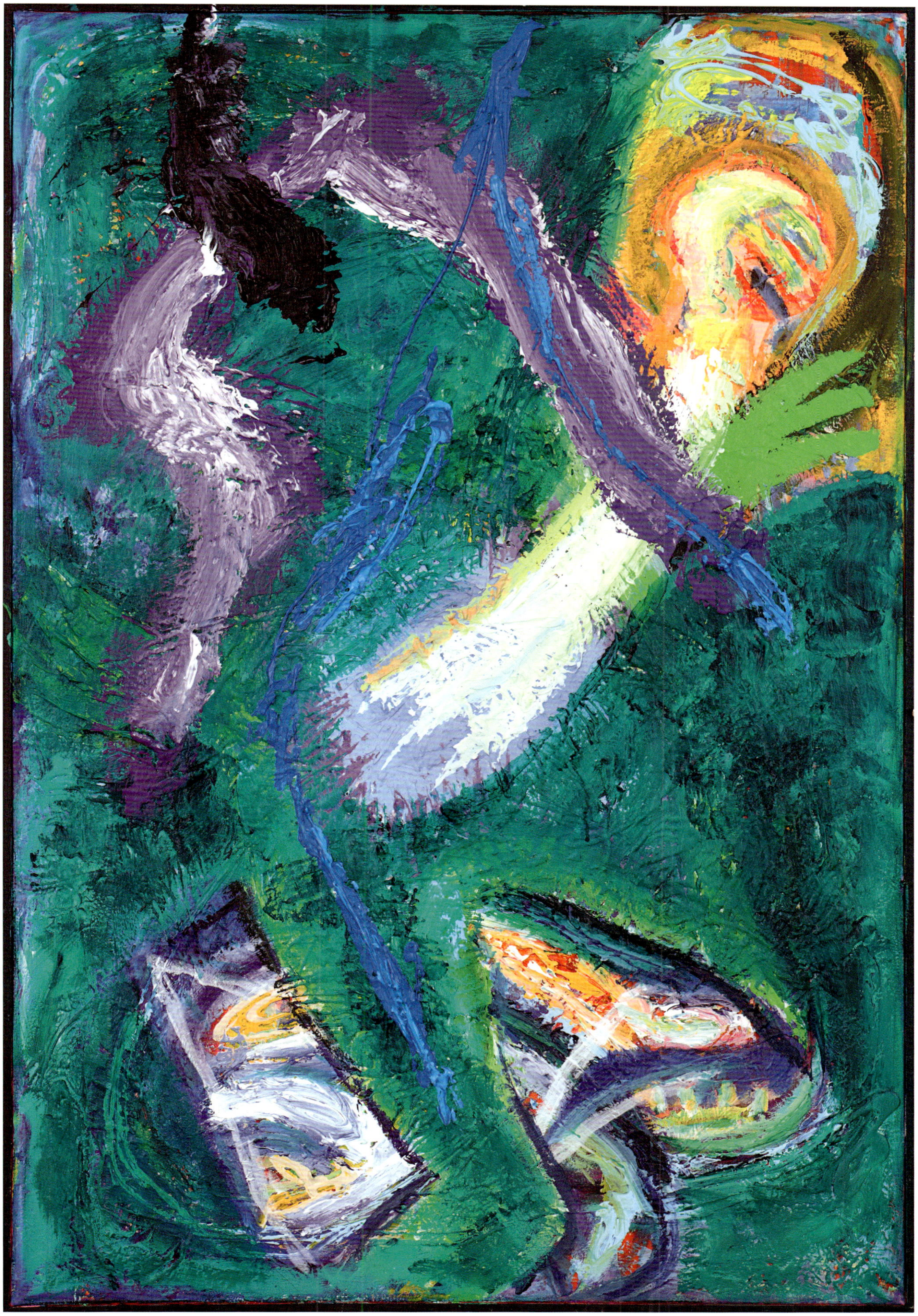

Children's Theatre
Kindertheater

2006
Acrylic on canvas, wooden battens, mounted / Acryl auf Leinwand, Holzleisten, montiert
78 × 56 cm

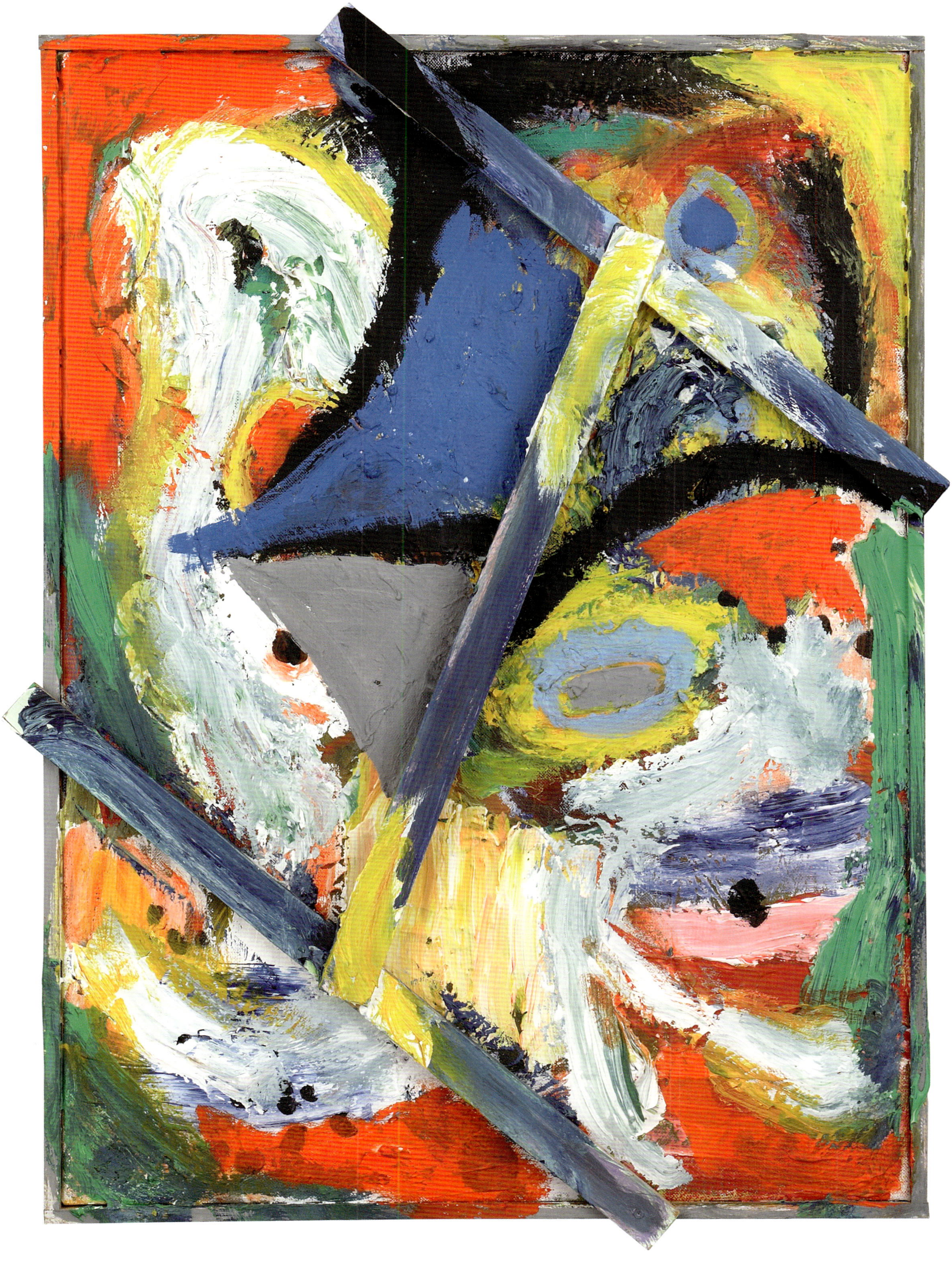

A Dream of a Step
... und macht im Traum den Schritt

1983/2010
Acrylic on three canvases, mounted / Acryl auf drei Leinwänden, montiert
241×170 cm

Schaub Collection / Sammlung Schaub

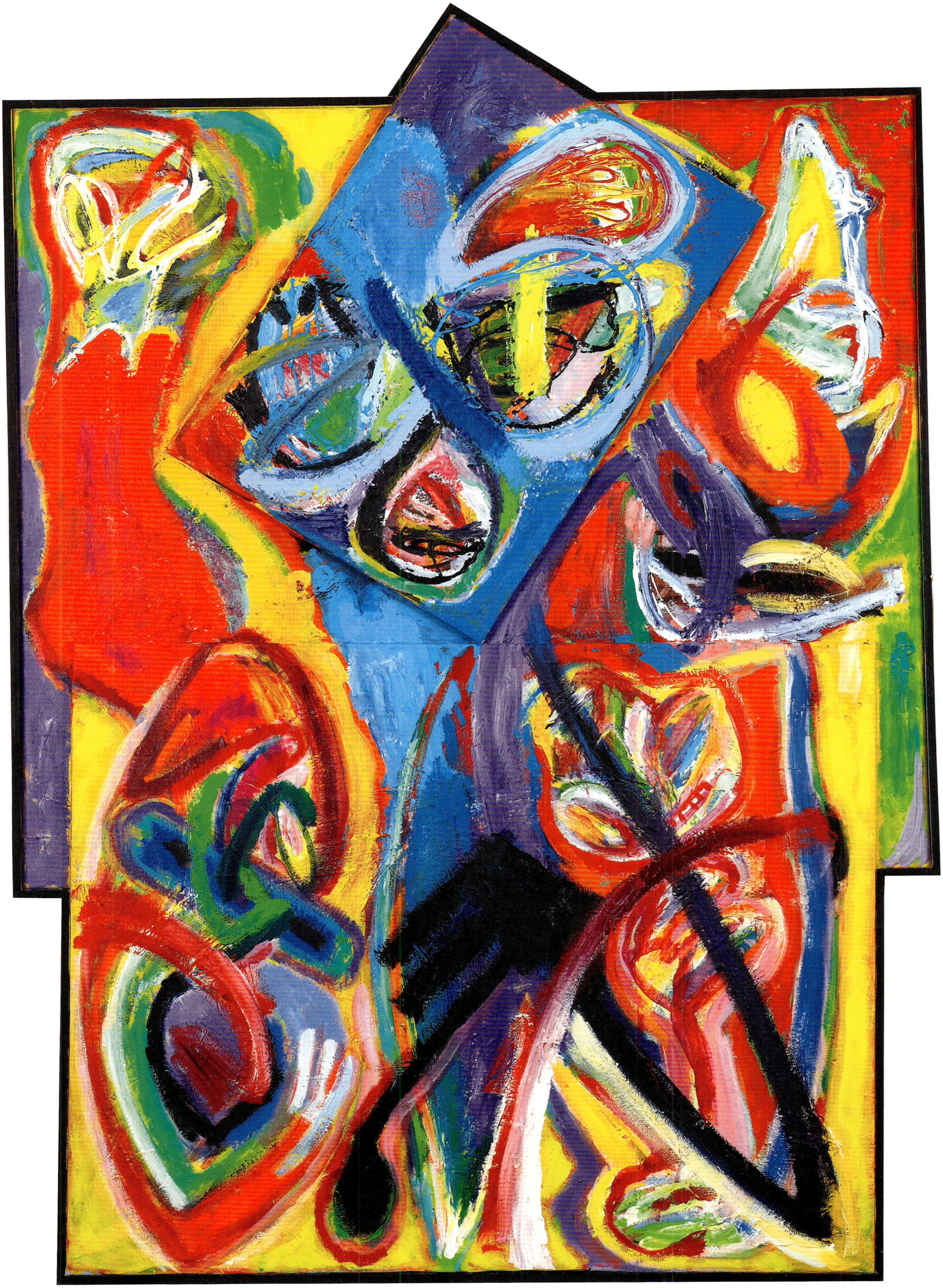

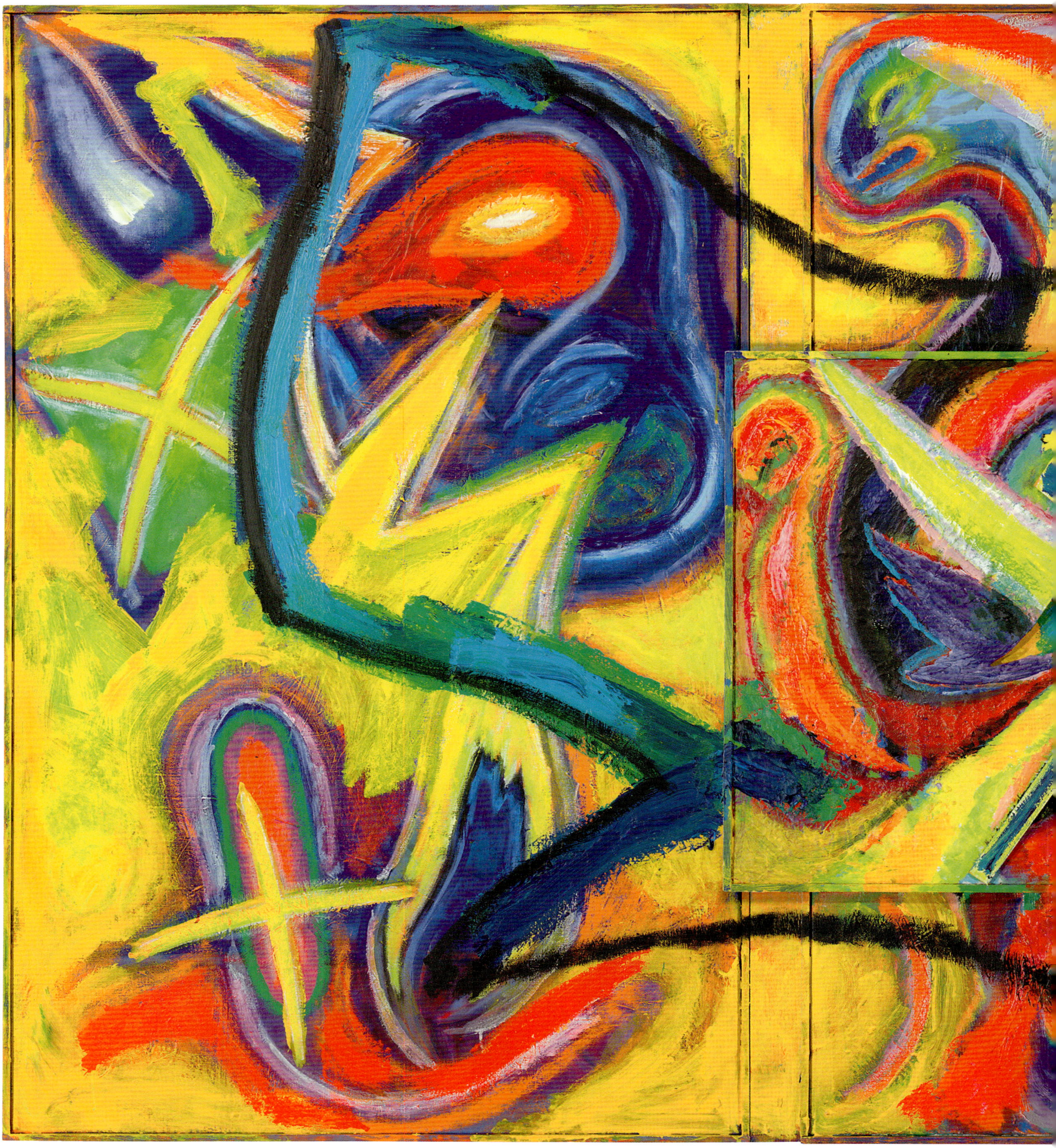

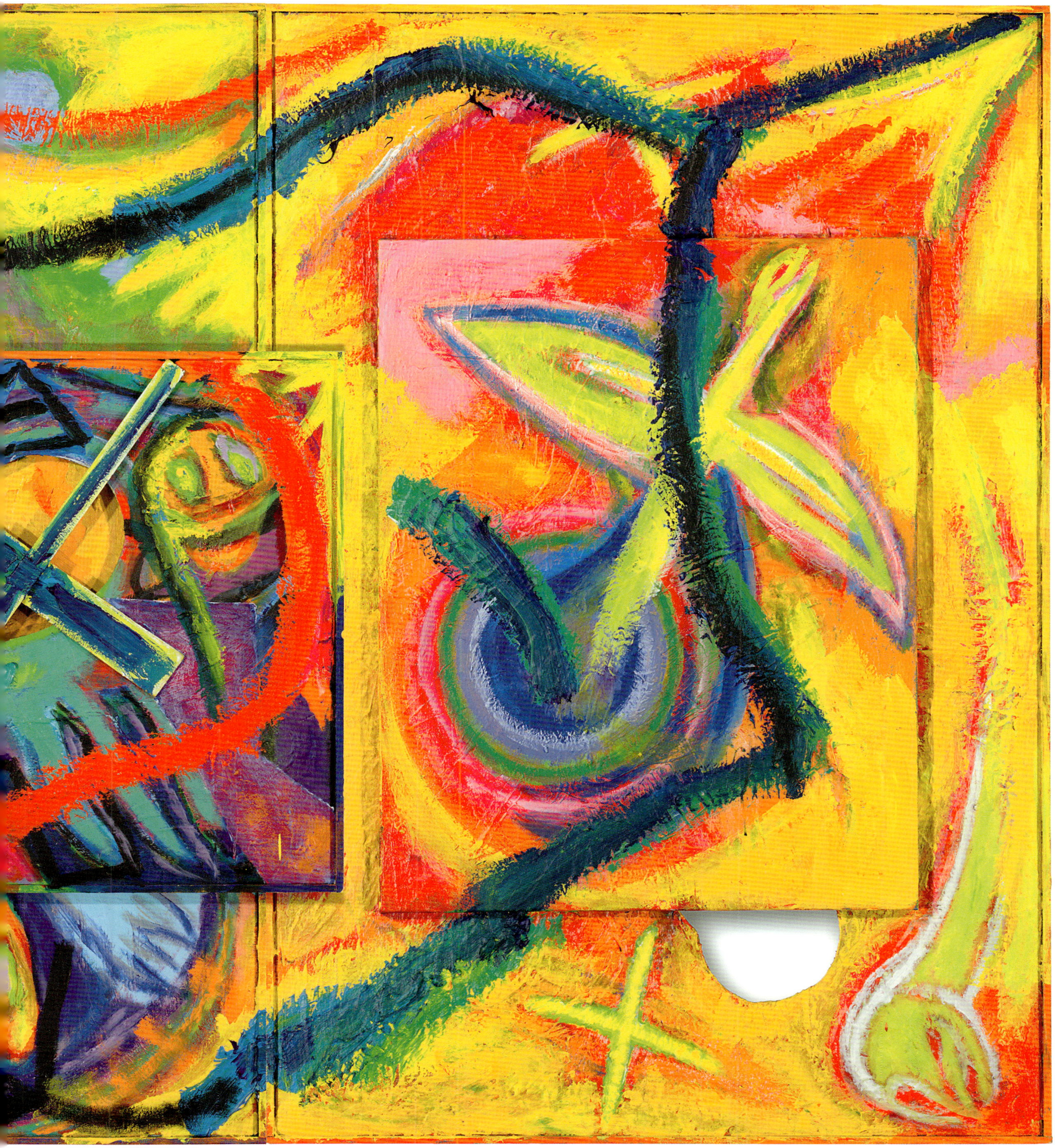

Page / Seite 40 – 41

The Birth of the Lion
Die Geburt des Löwen

1999/2001/2010
Three-part, acrylic on four canvases and one hardboard sheet, mounted, fixed wooden cross
3-teilig, Acryl auf vier Leinwänden und einer Pressspanplatte, montiert, Applikation Holzkreuz
153 × 280 cm

Form Frees
Form befreit

2008
Acrylic on three canvases, wooden frame and wooden batten, mounted and cut
Acryl auf drei Leinwänden, Holzrahmen und Holzleisten, montiert und geschnitten
180 × 150 cm

HRH Duke Franz of Bavaria Collection / Sammlung SKH Herzog Franz von Bayern

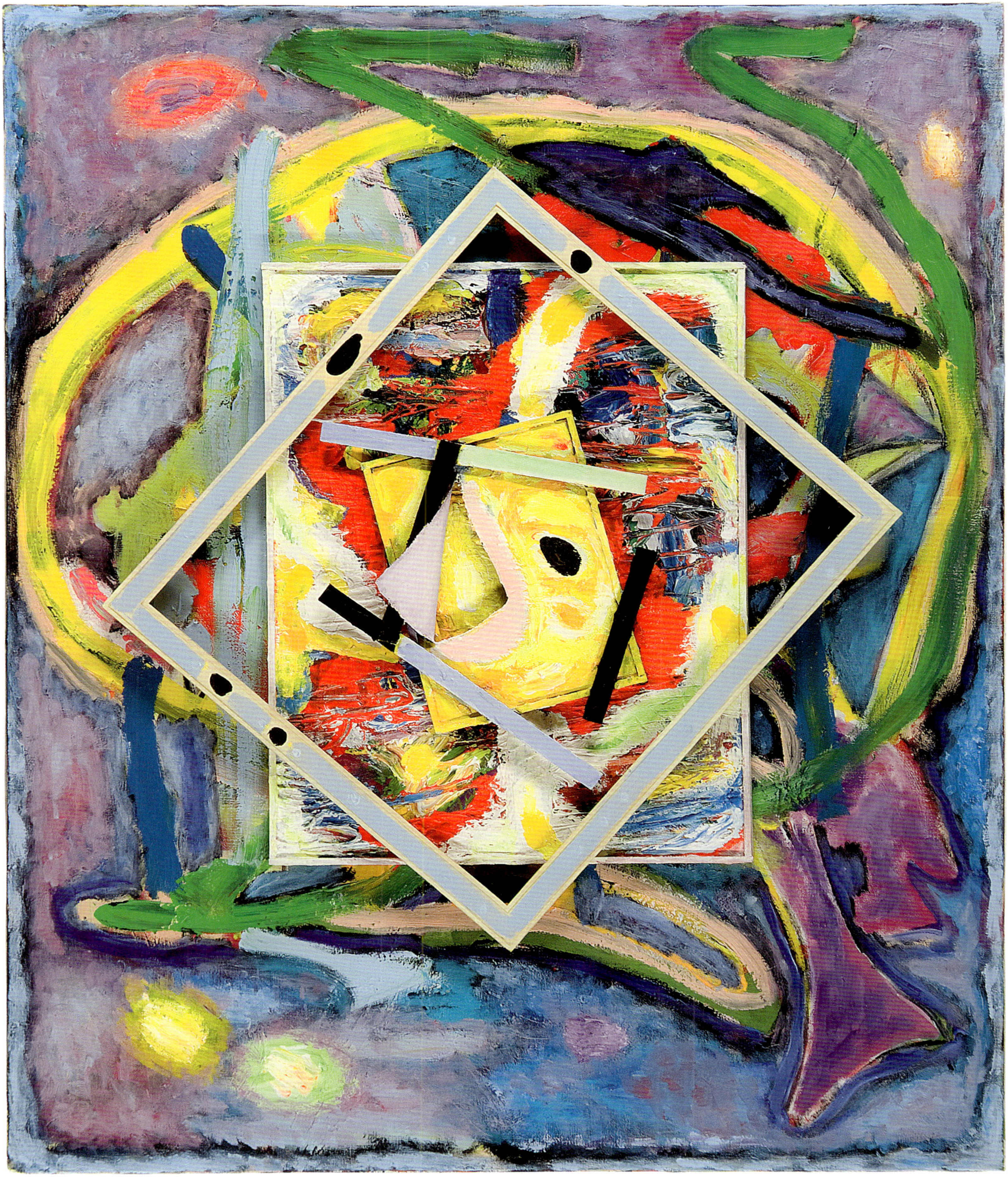

2007

Donkey's Ear
Eselsohr

2007
Acrylic on canvas / Acryl auf Leinwand
102 × 82 cm

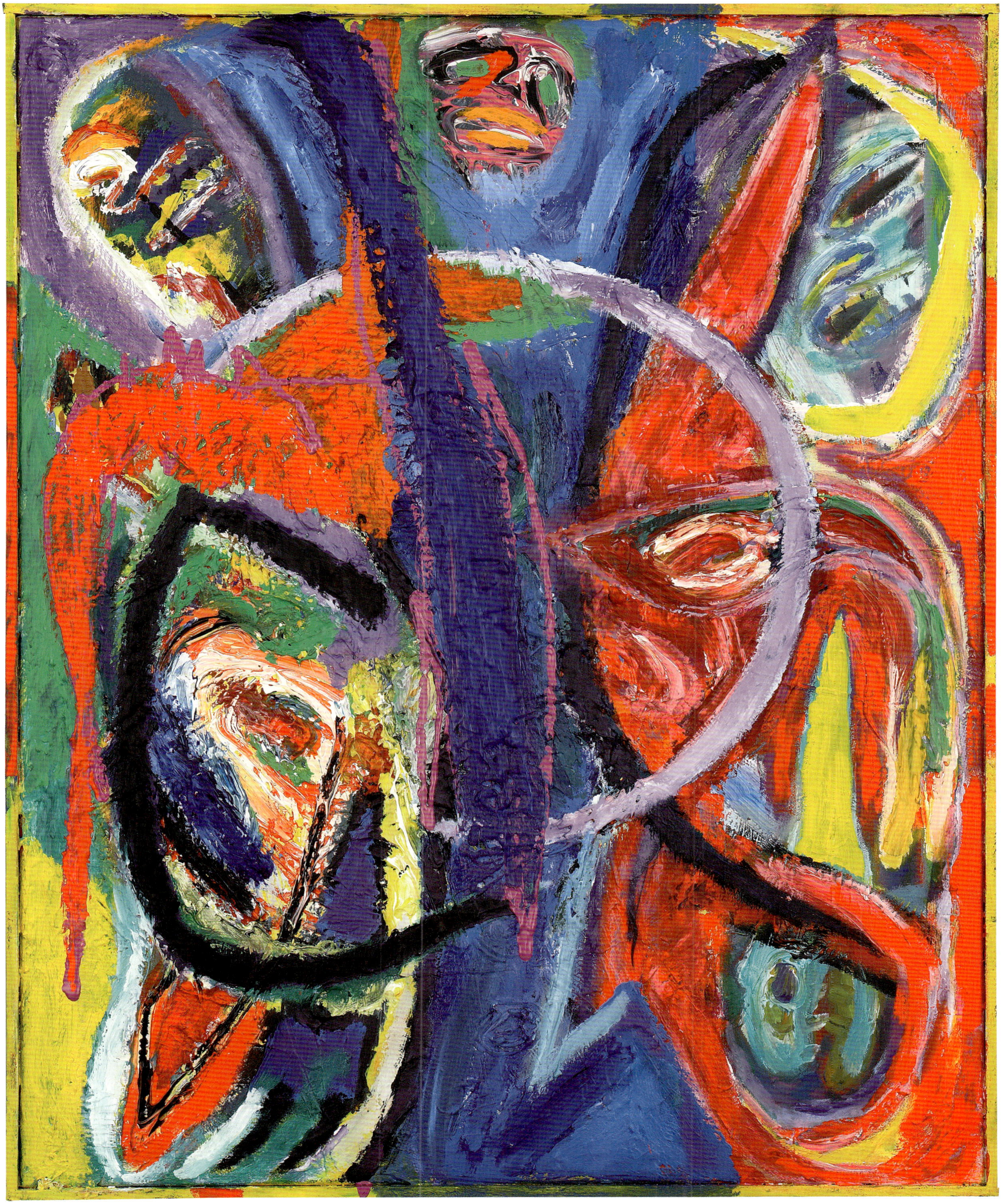

Feather
Feder

2006/2011
Acrylic on plywood / Acryl auf Sperrholz
165 × 114 cm

Schick Collection / Sammlung Schick

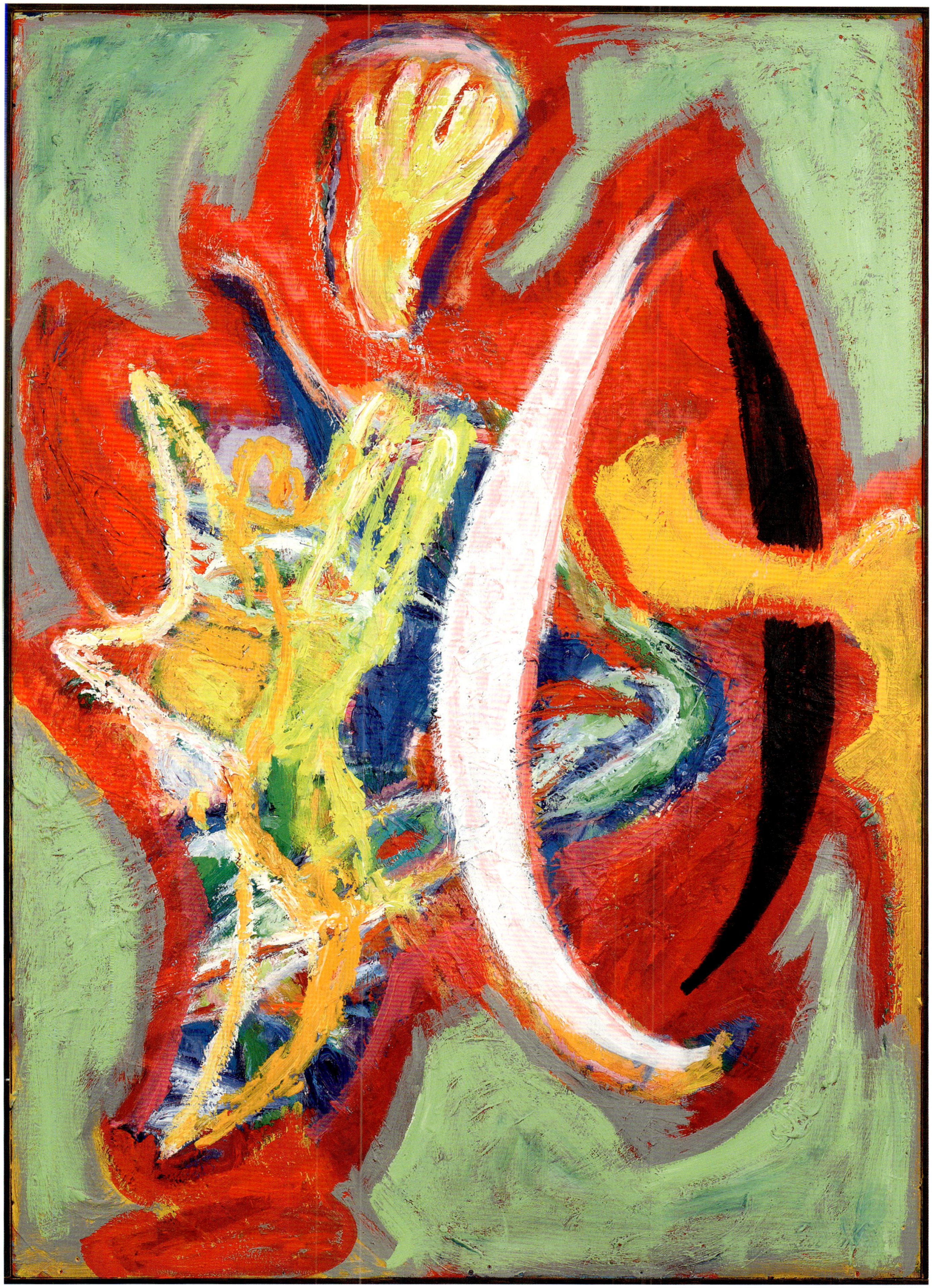

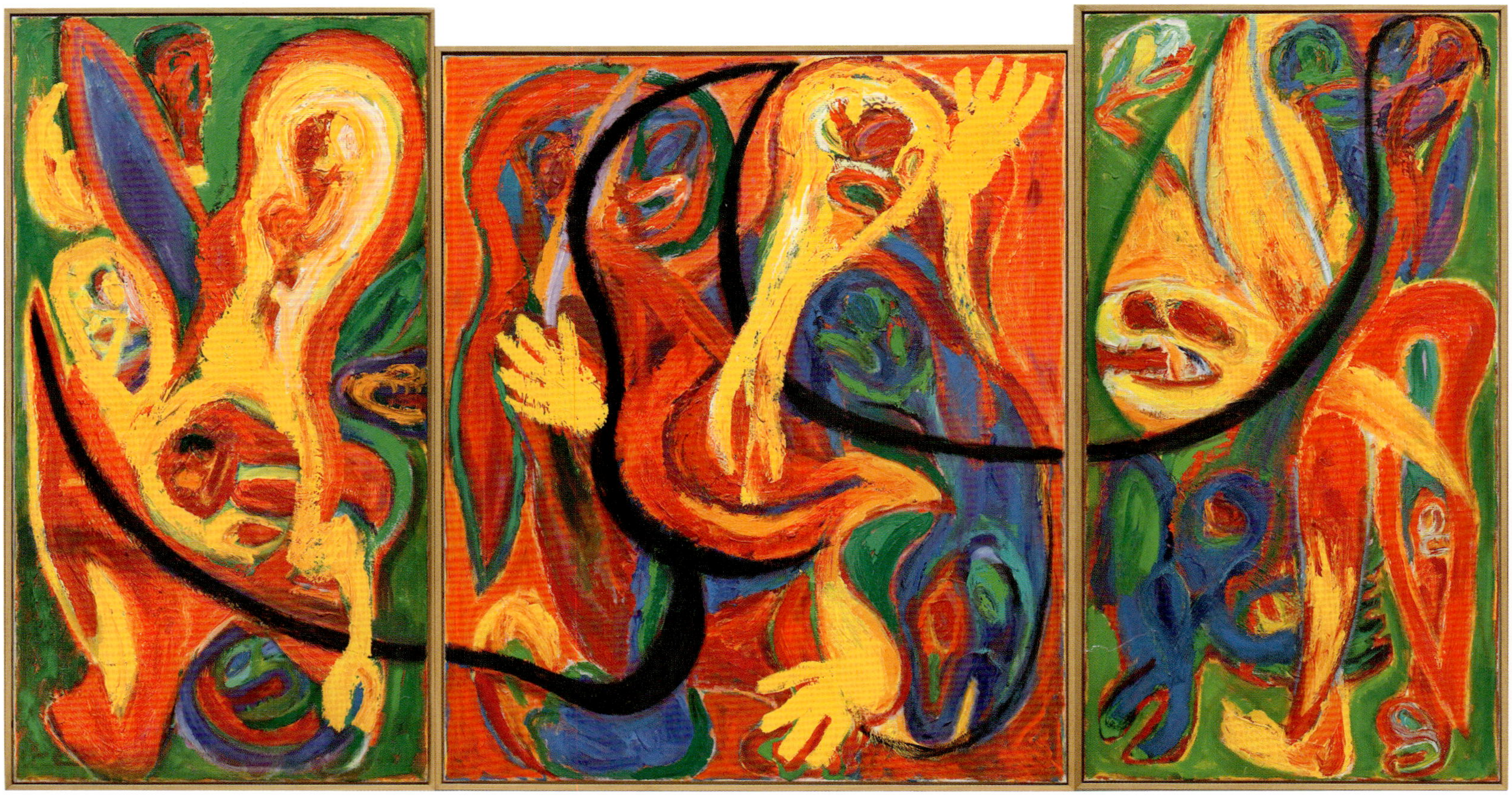

The Dance
Der Tanz

1995
Triptych, acrylic on canvas / Triptychon, Acryl auf Leinwand
194 × 364 cm

Schaub Collection / Sammlung Schaub

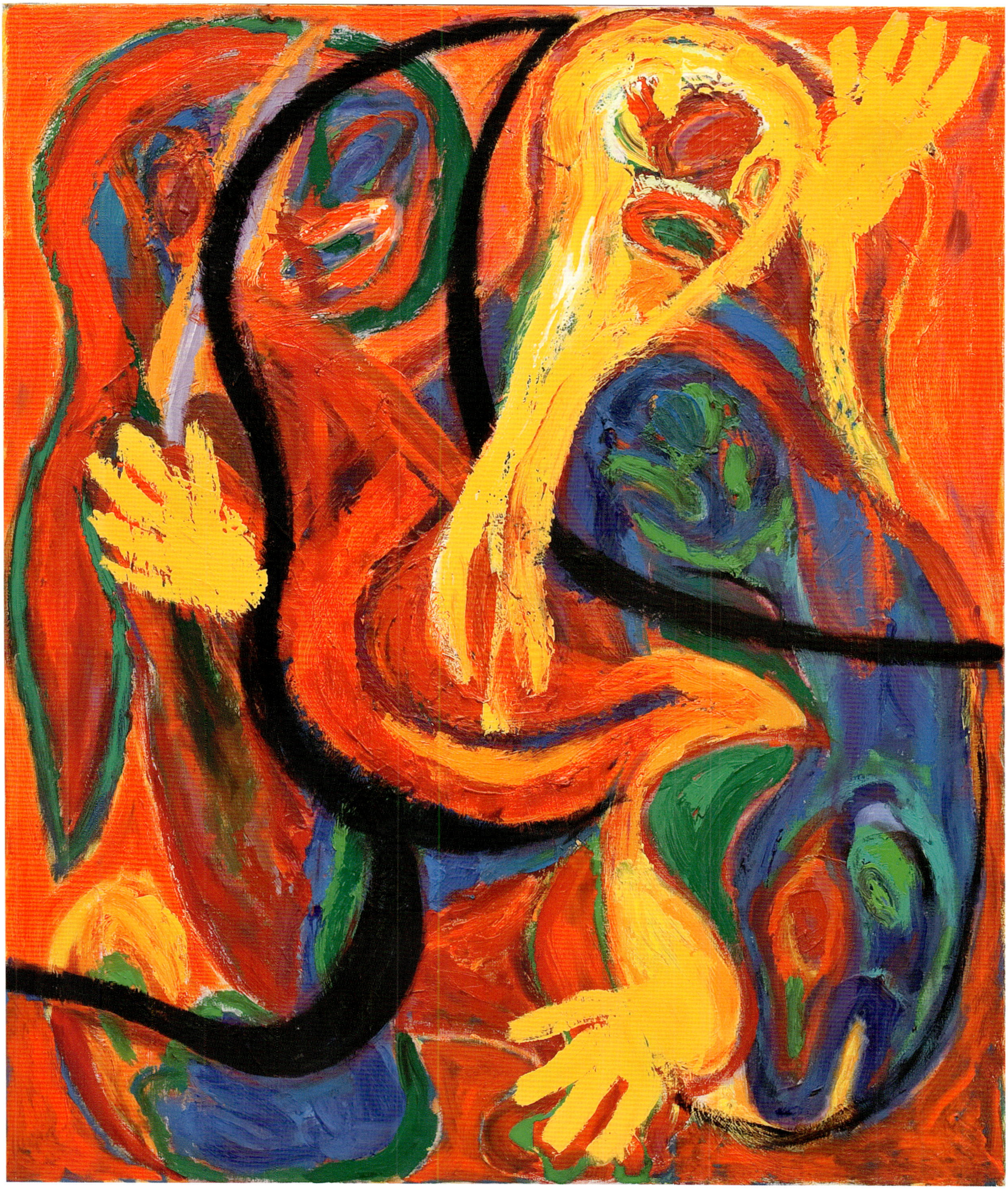

Every Angel Is Dreadful
Ein jeder Engel ist schrecklich

1996/2000/2004/2006
Acrylic on canvas / Acryl auf Leinwand
102 × 72 cm

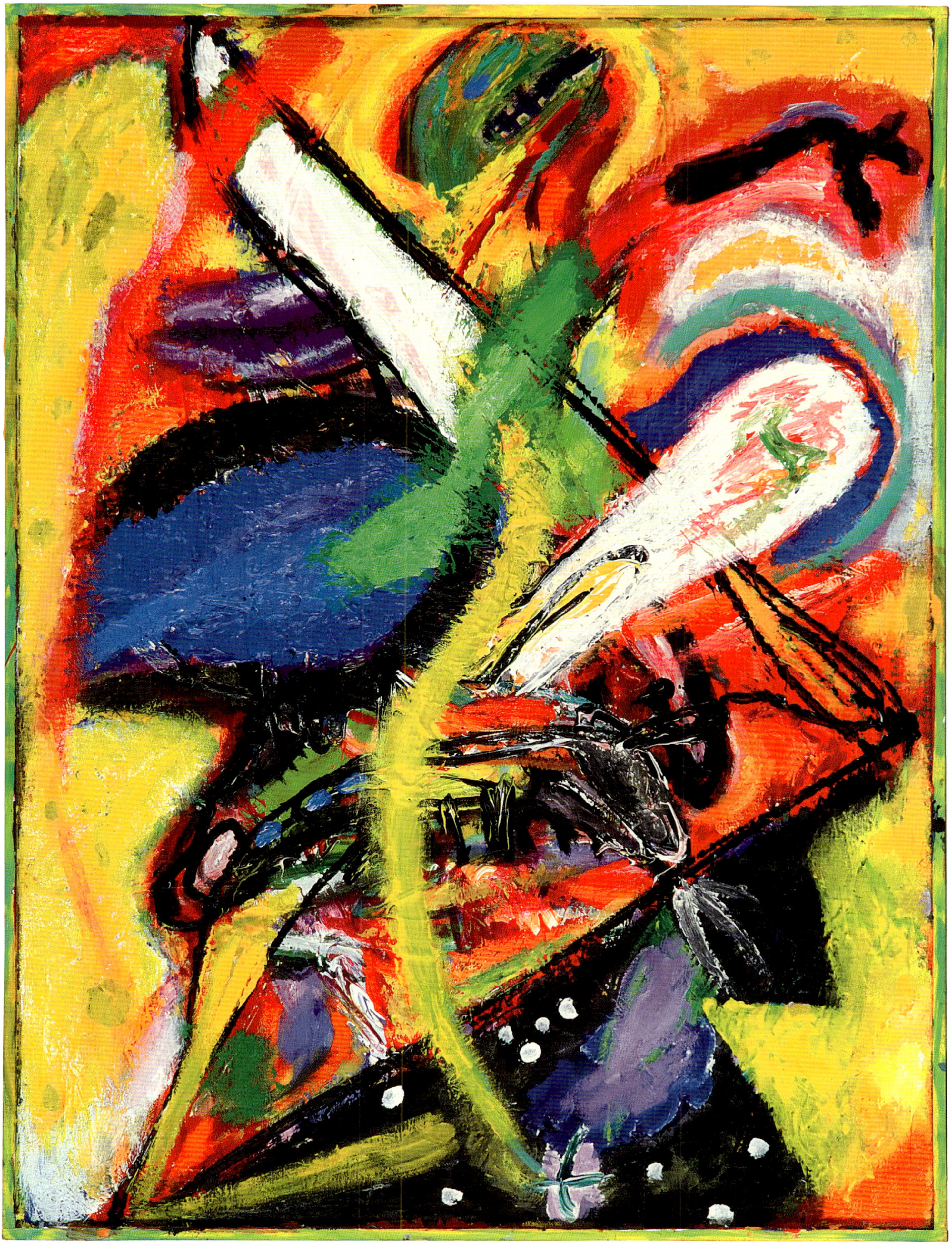

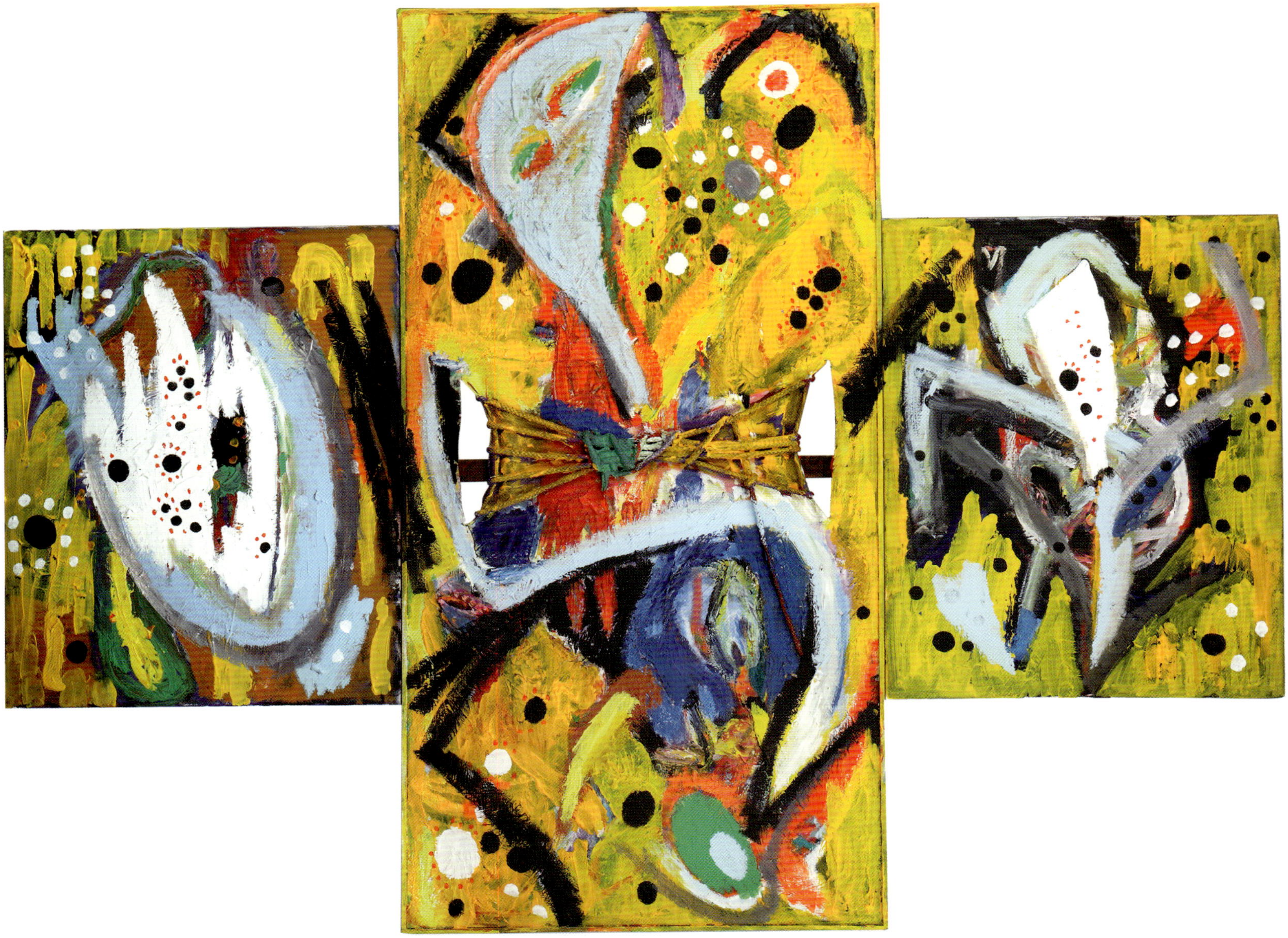

Cross, Bound
Kreuz, geschnürt

2006
Acrylic on three canvases, mounted and cut / Acryl auf drei Leinwänden, montiert und geschnitten
190 × 256 cm

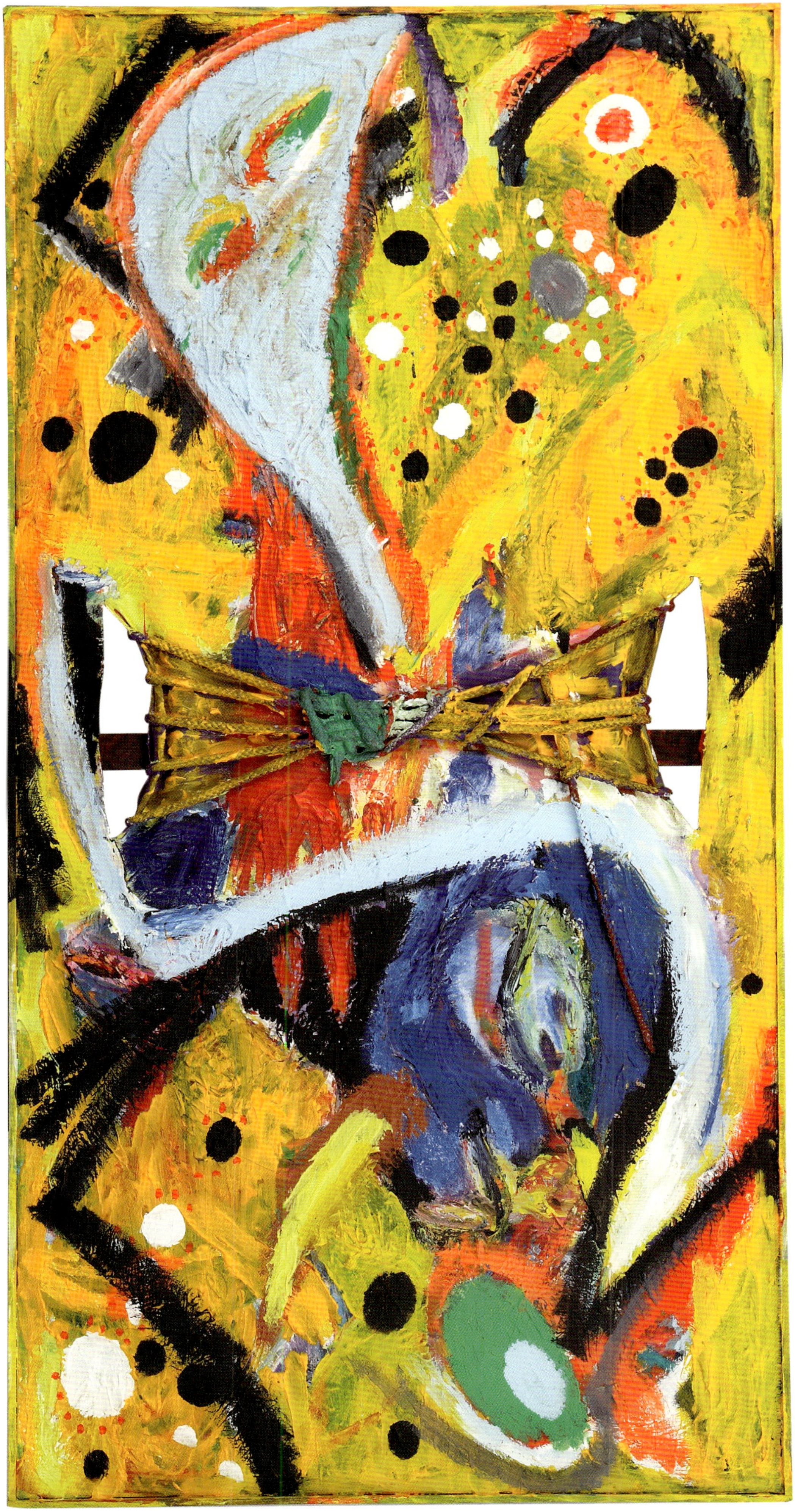

Knock My Head Off!
Schlag mir den Kopf ab!

2000/2010
Acrylic on hardboard / Acryl auf Hartfaserplatte
99 × 72 cm

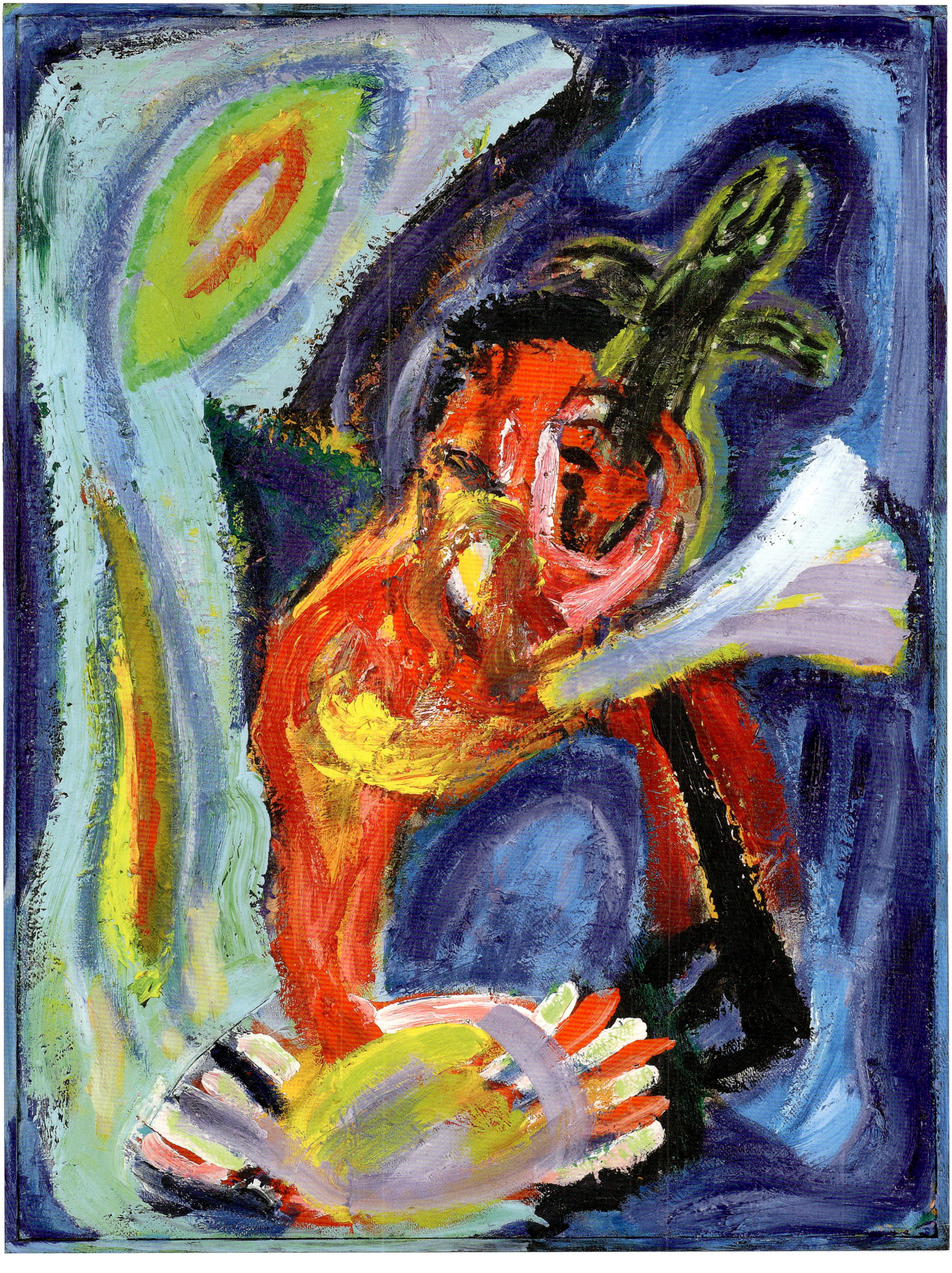

Chronos
Chronos

2007
Acrylic on canvas / Acryl auf Leinwand
95 × 130 cm

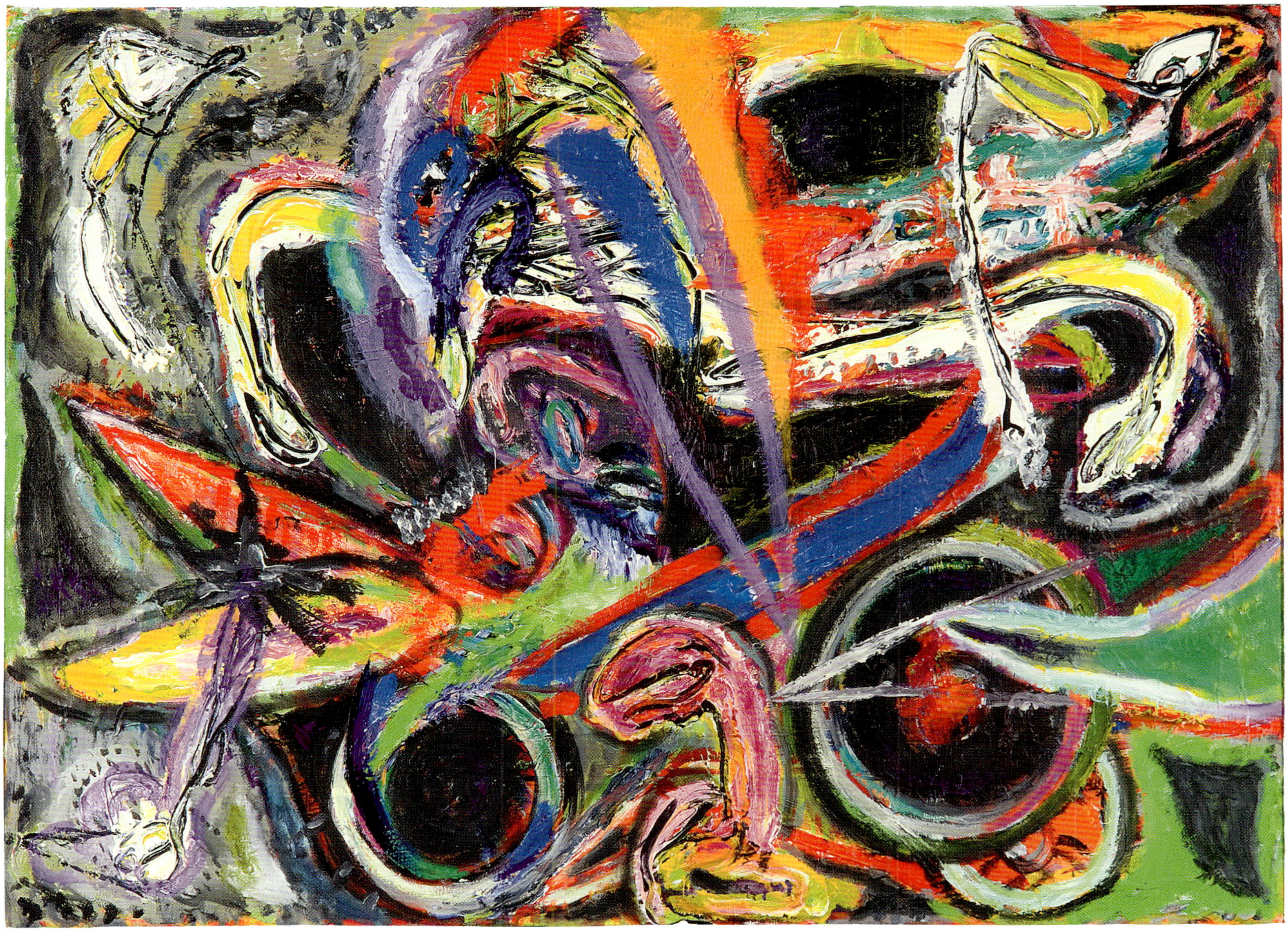

The Grasper
Der Begreifer

2007
Acrylic on canvas / Acryl auf Leinwand
85 × 65 cm

Private collection, Cham / Privatsammlung Cham

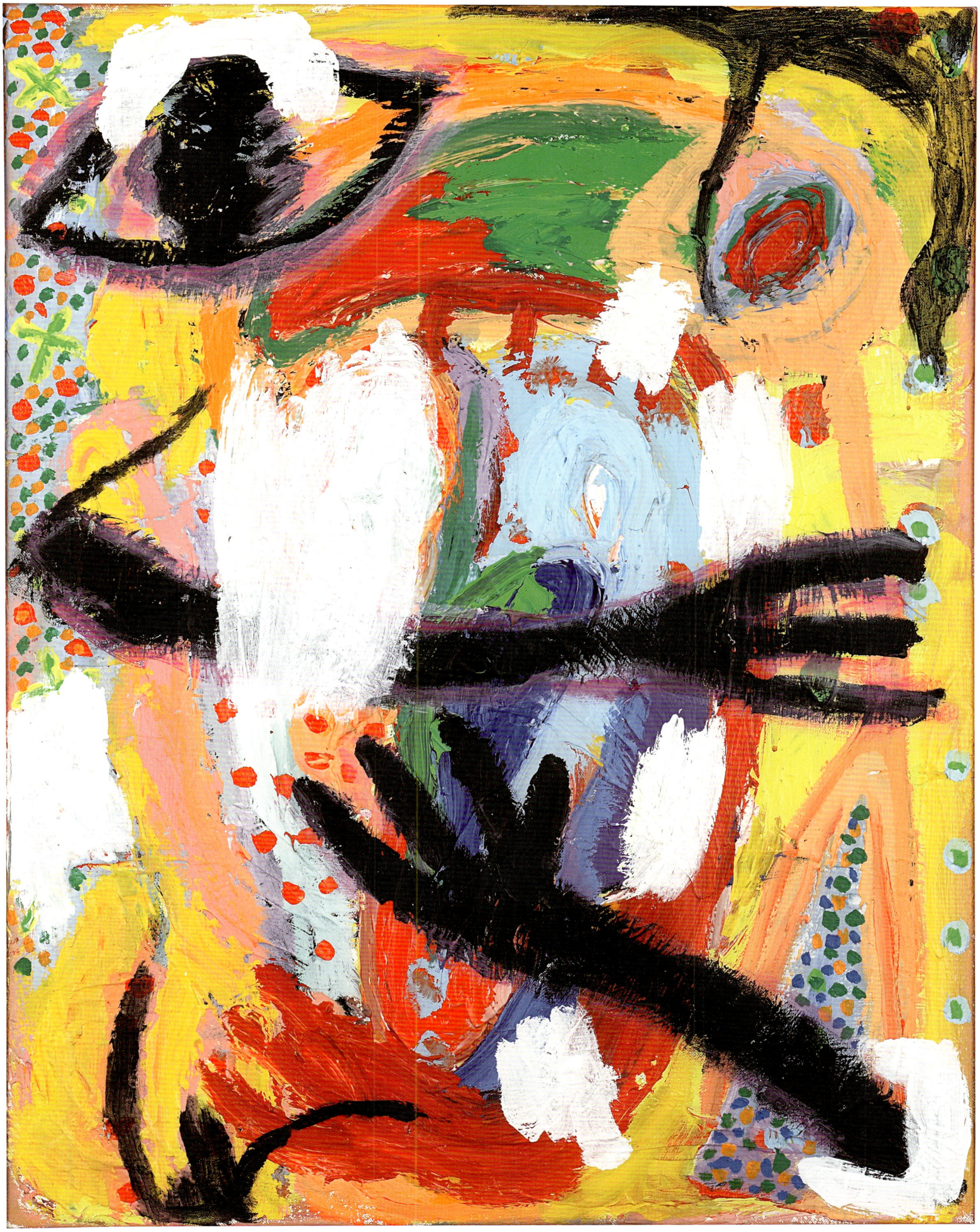

Outlawed
Vogelfrei

2012
Acrylic on canvas / Acryl auf Leinwand
100 × 70 cm

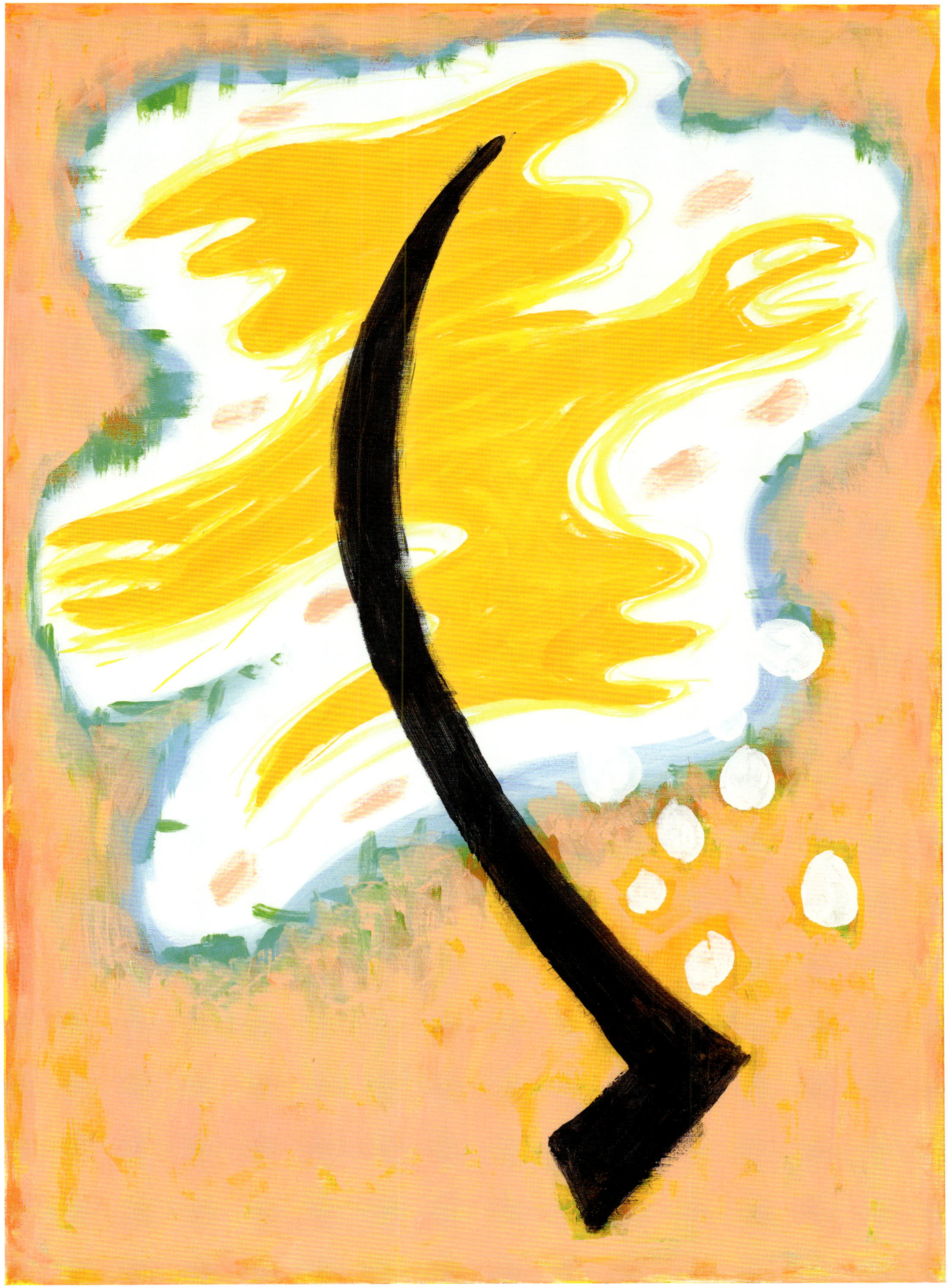

Cross
Kreuz

2008/2009
Acrylic on hardboard, two canvases, mounted / Acryl auf Hartfaserplatten, zwei Leinwände, montiert
206 × 221 cm

HRH Duke Franz of Bavaria Collection / Sammlung SKH Herzog Franz von Bayern

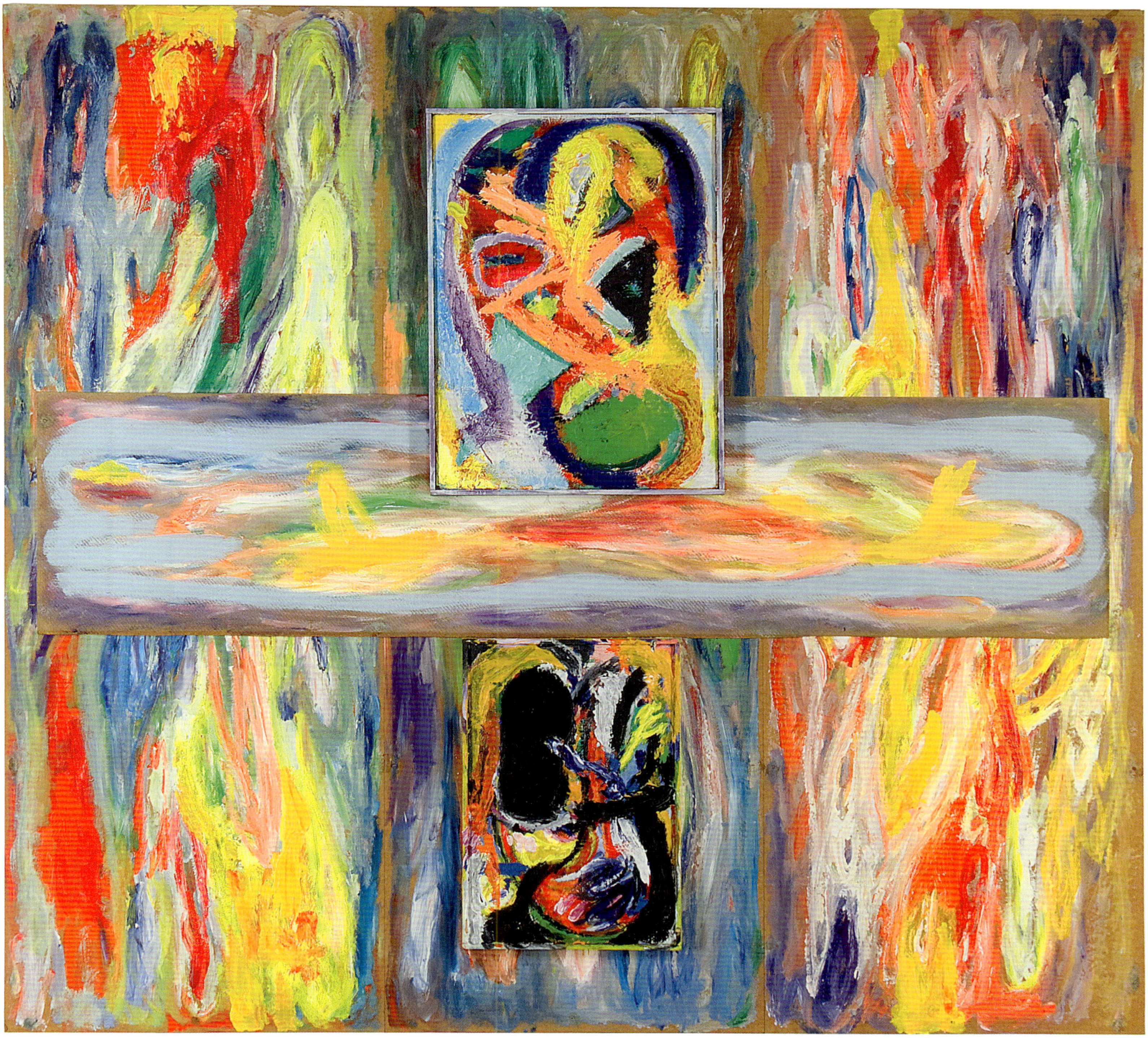

The Yellow Spot Changed It All
Die Schuld des gelben Flecks an der Verwandlung

2006
Acrylic on canvas / Acryl auf Leinwand
82 × 62 cm

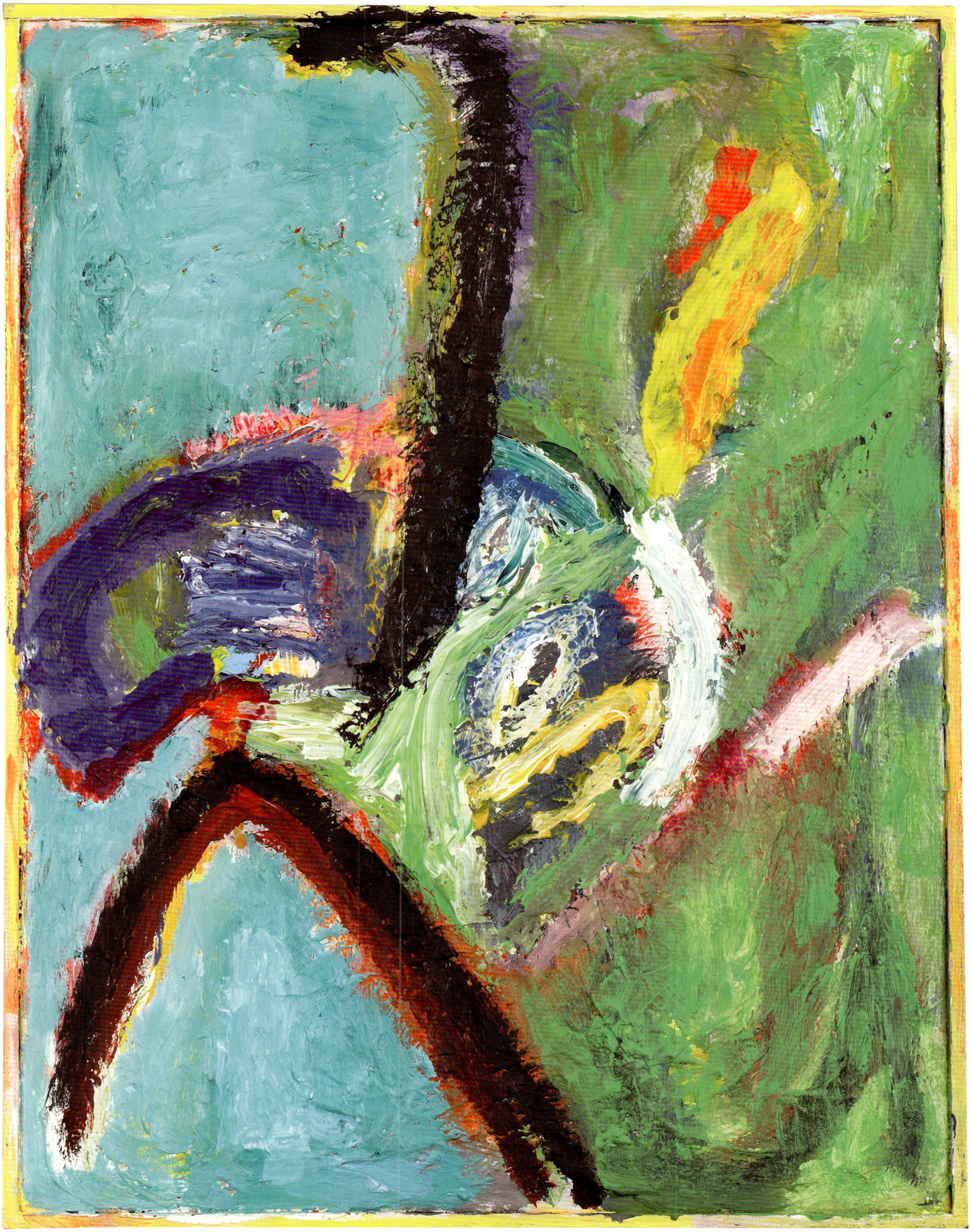

Membrane
Membran

2012
Acrylic on canvas / Acryl auf Leinwand
100 × 70 cm
Galerie Biedermann, München

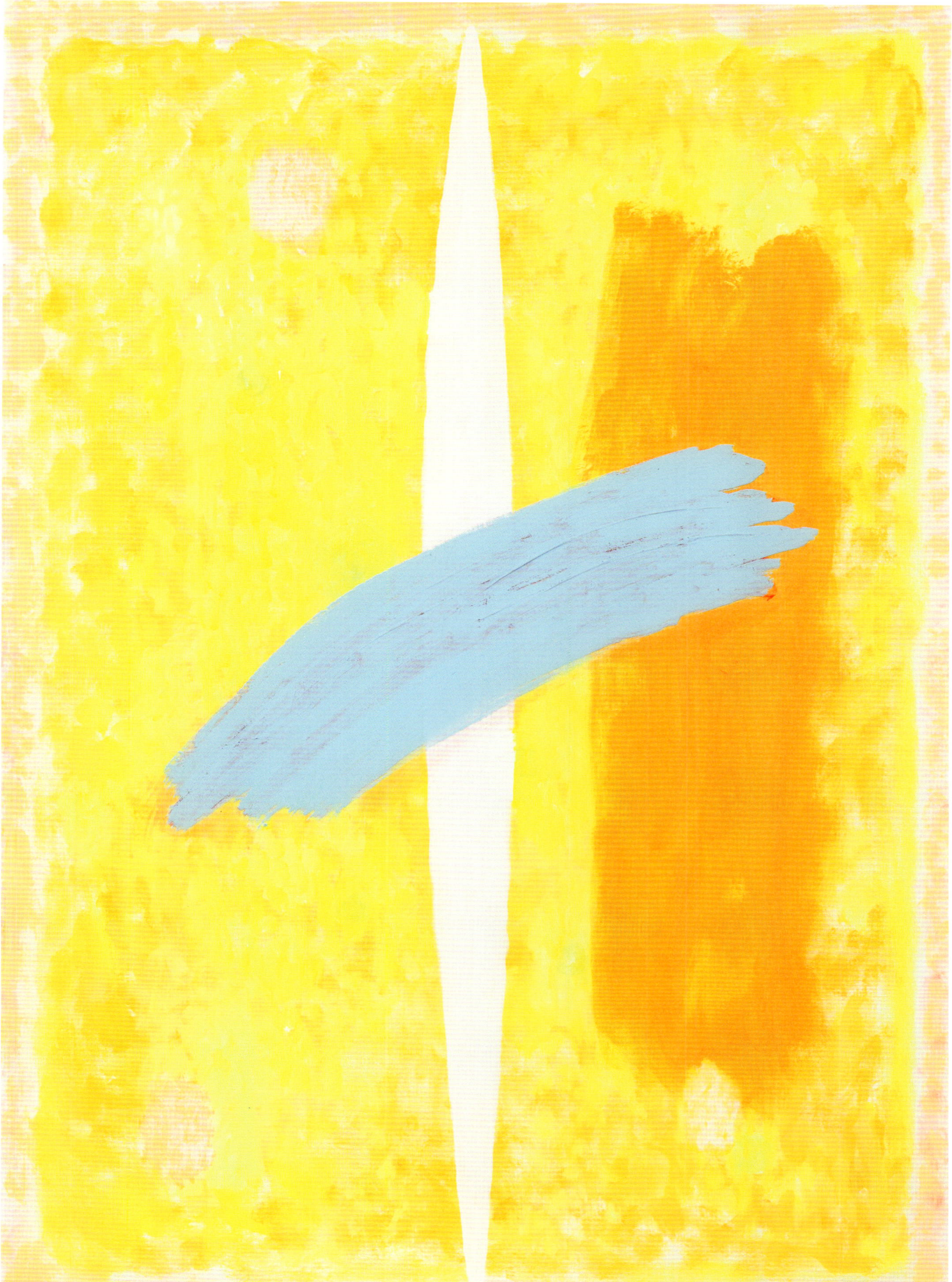

Salire
Salire

1992/2009/2012
Acrylic on canvas, plywood and wooden battens, mounted / Acryl auf Leinwand, Holzspanplatten und Holzleisten, montiert
236 × 171 cm

HRH Duke Franz of Bavaria Collection / Sammlung SKH Herzog Franz von Bayern

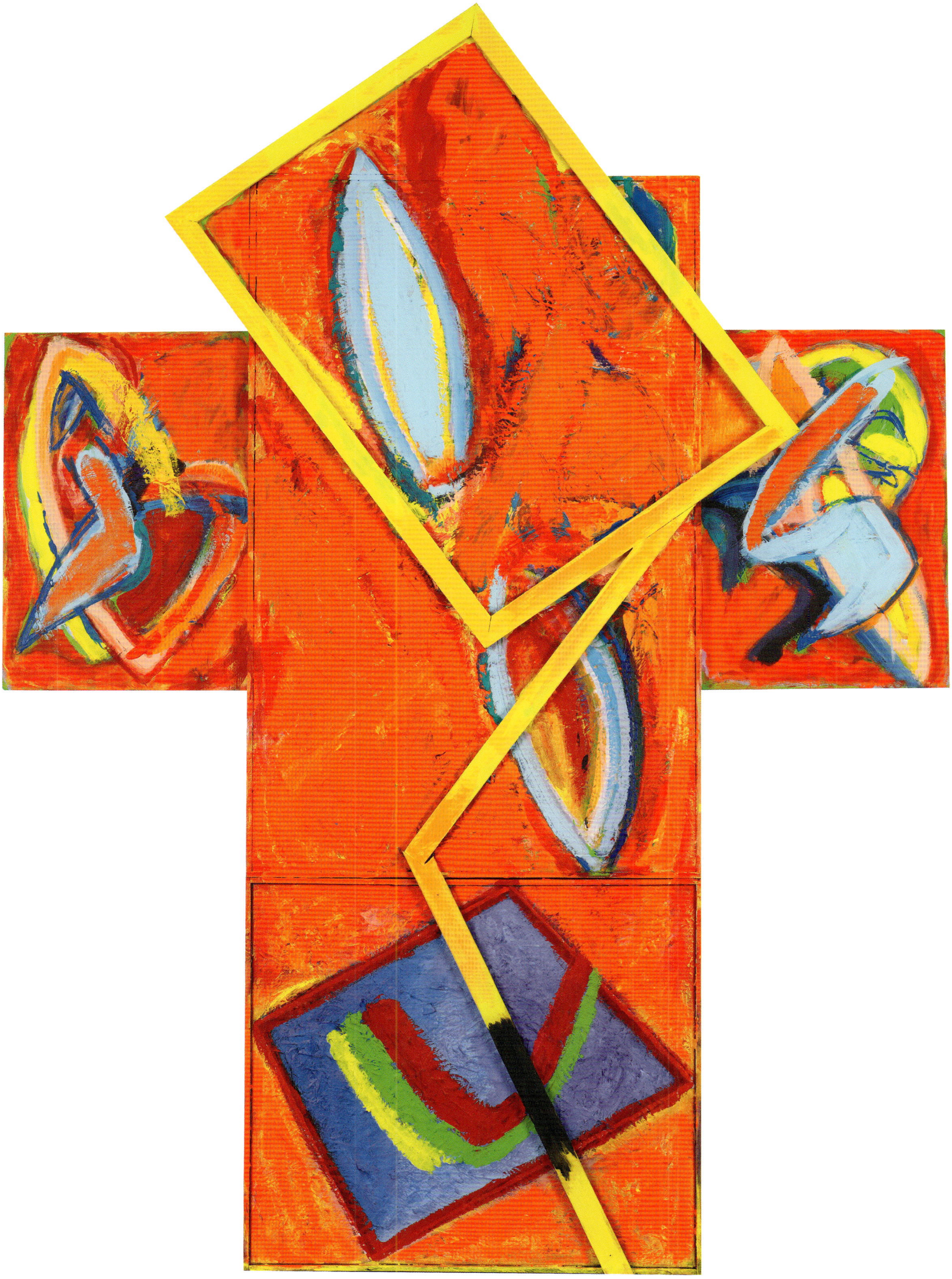

Expansion
Expansion

2005
Acrylic on canvas / Acryl auf Leinwand
82 × 82 cm

Private collection / Privatsammlung

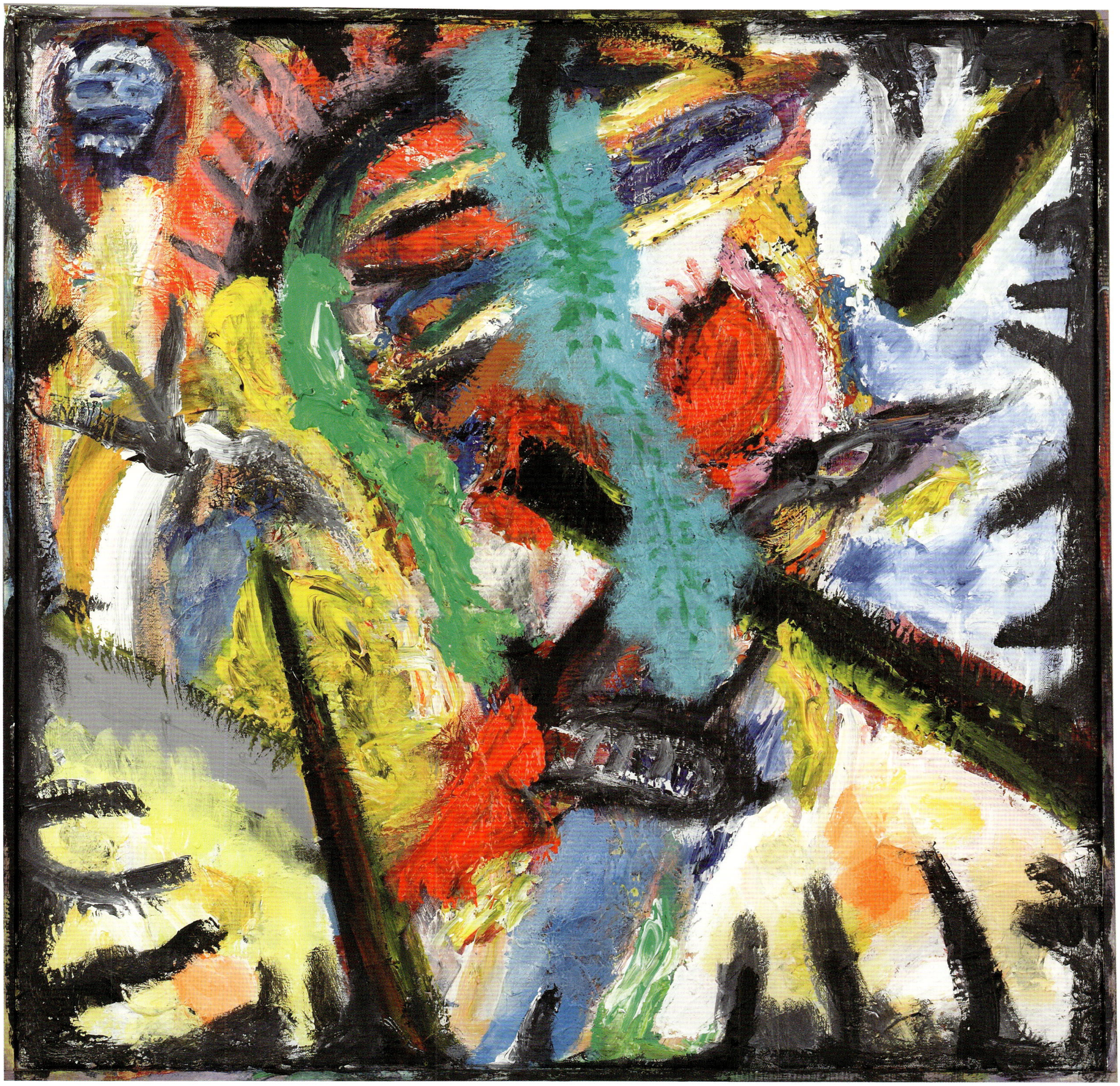

Flash of Lightning
Lichtschlag

2012
Acrylic on canvas / Acryl auf Leinwand
82 × 102 cm

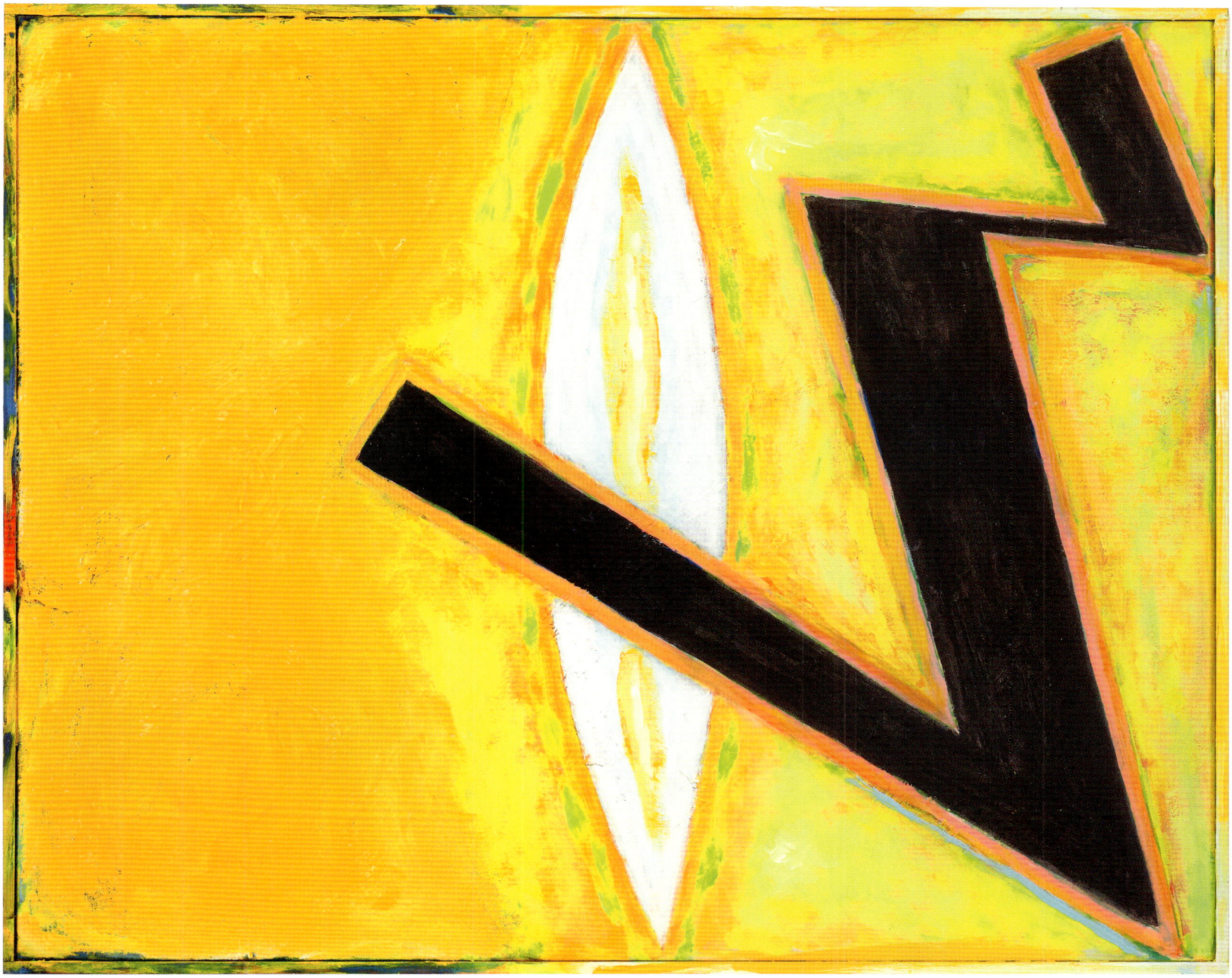

Envelopment
Umfassung

2005
Acrylic on canvas / Acryl auf Leinwand
82 × 72 cm

Kurt Schäfer Collection / Sammlung Kurt Schäfer

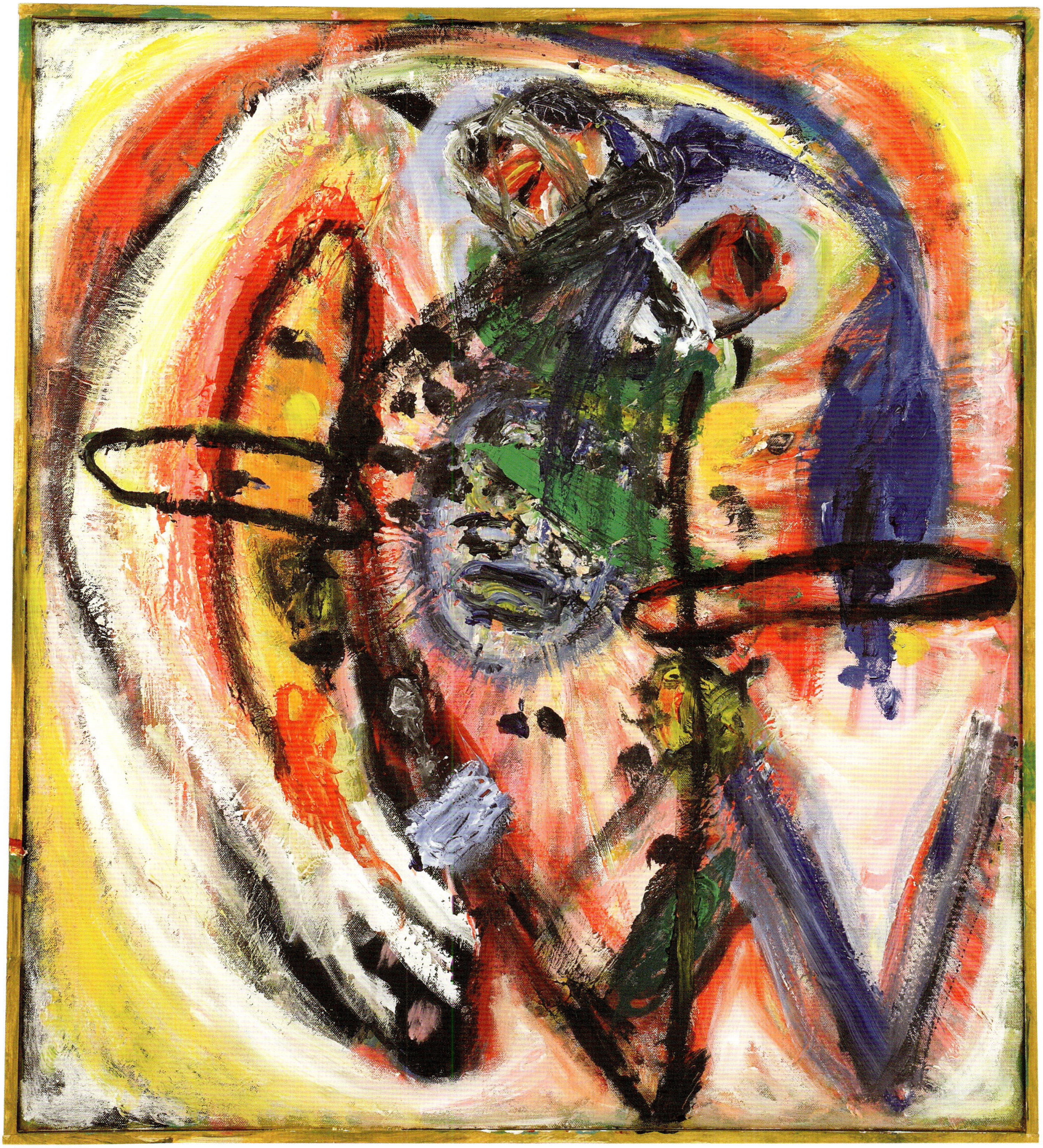

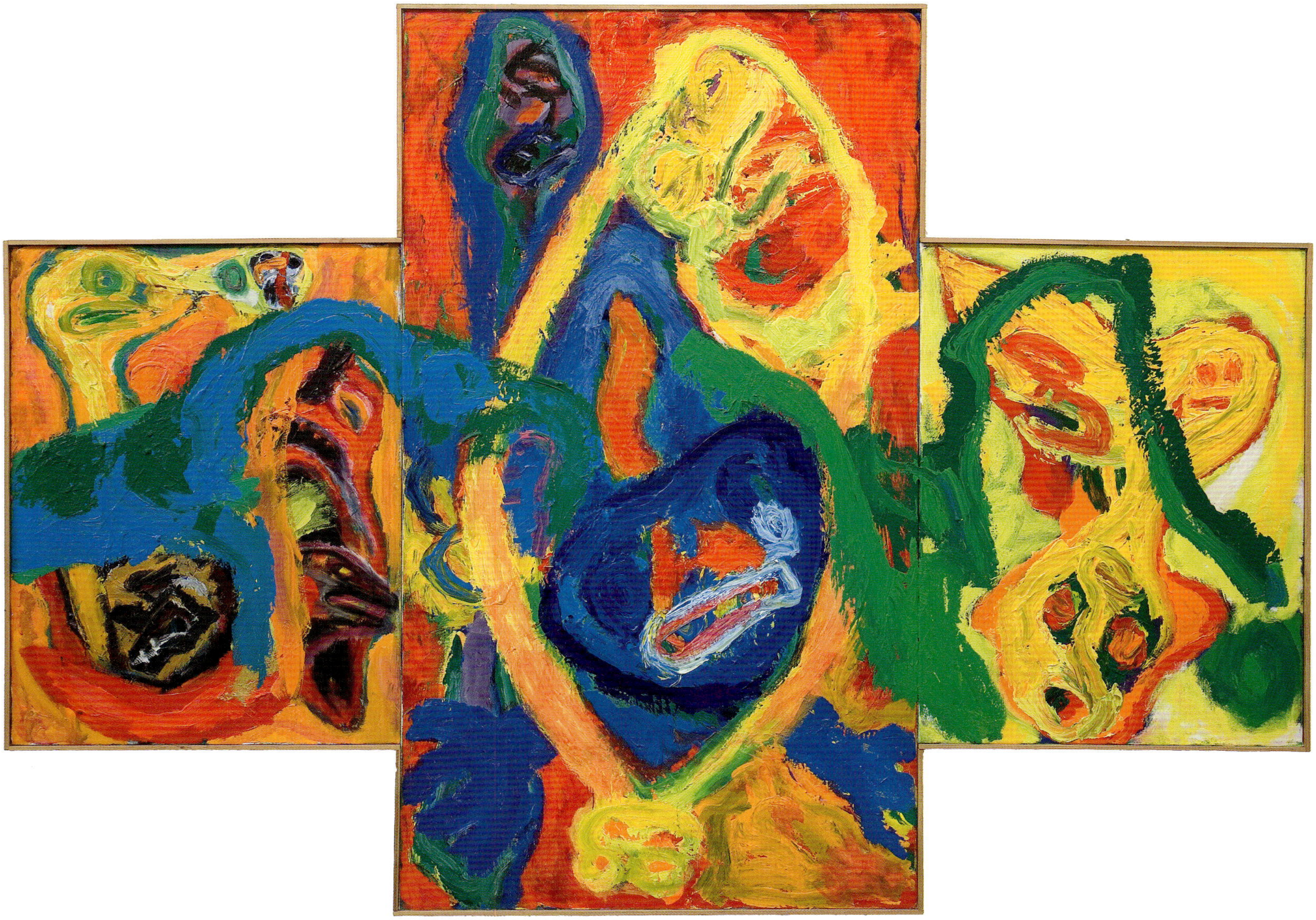

Limelight
Im Licht

1992
Acrylic on three canvases, mounted / Acryl auf drei Leinwänden, montiert
179.5 × 250 cm / 179,5 × 250 cm

Schick Collection / Sammlung Schick

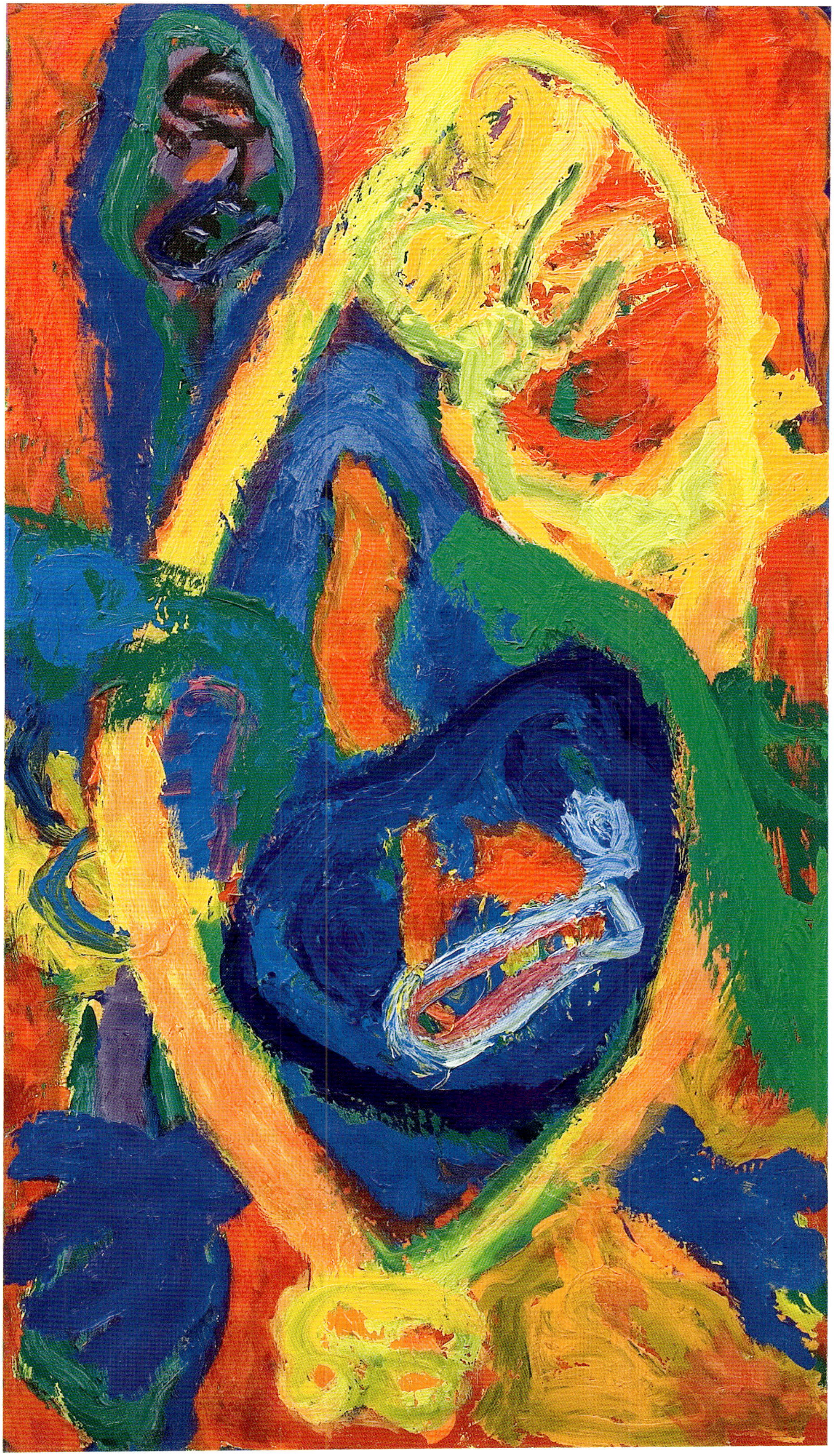

No Place
Kein Ort

1992/1999/2010
Acrylic on canvas / Acryl auf Leinwand
152 × 122 cm

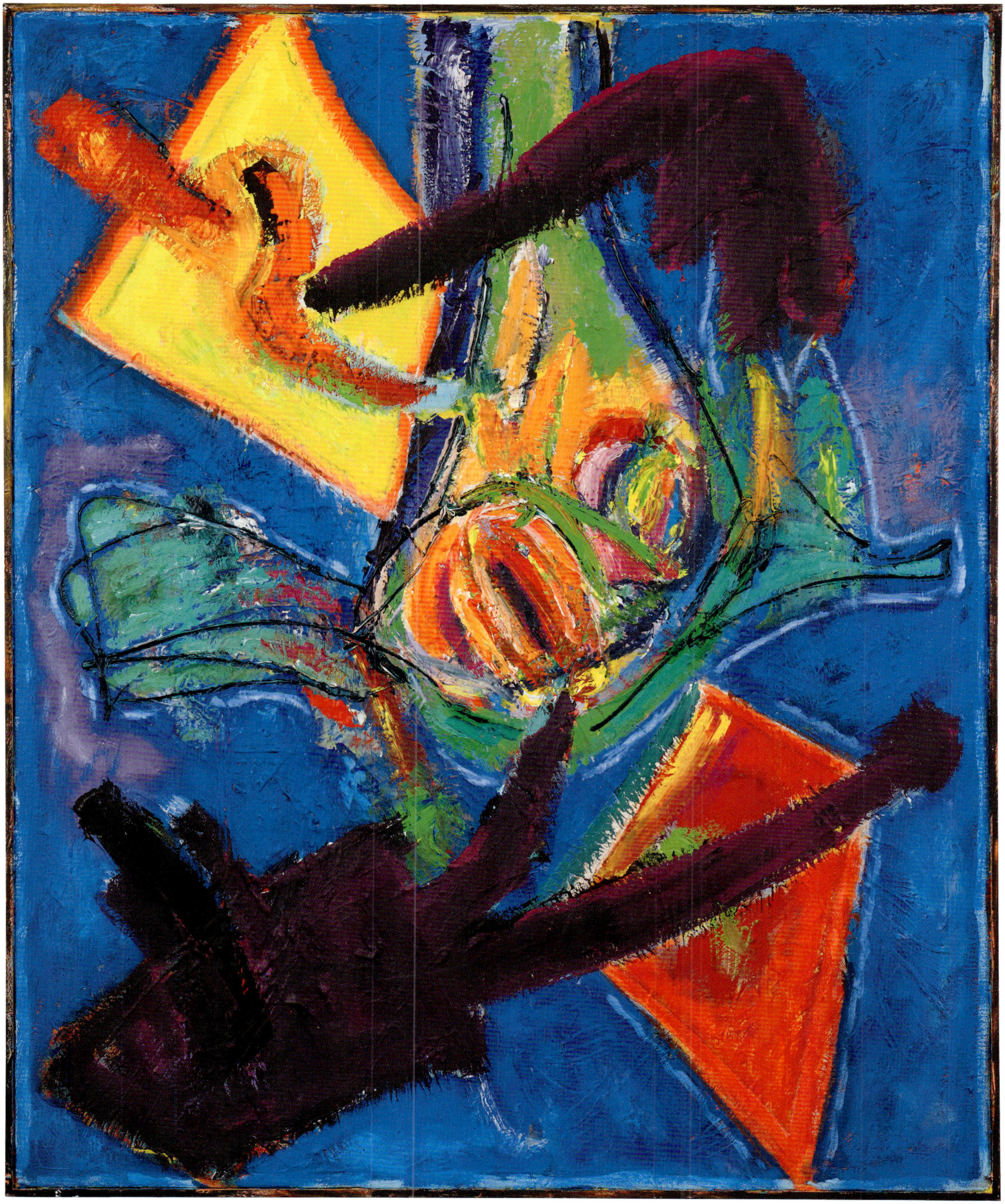

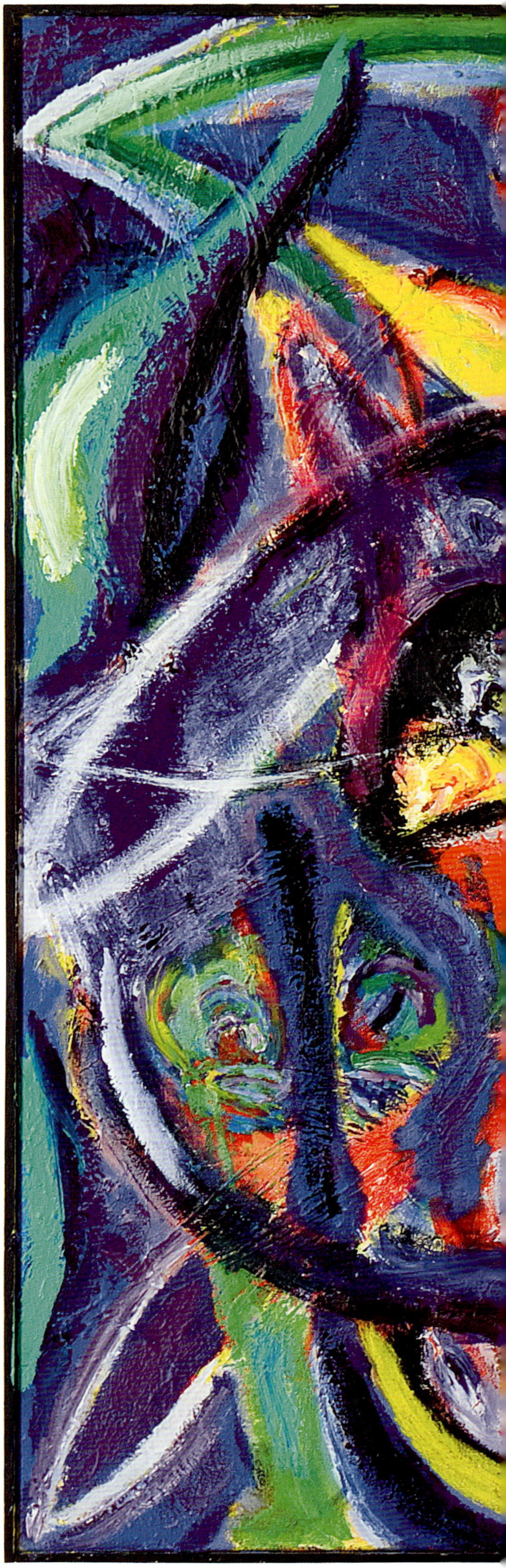

Yearning for Colour
Die Sehnsucht der Farben

2005/2006/2007
Acrylic on canvas / Acryl auf Leinwand
154 × 184 cm

Schaub Collection / Sammlung Schaub

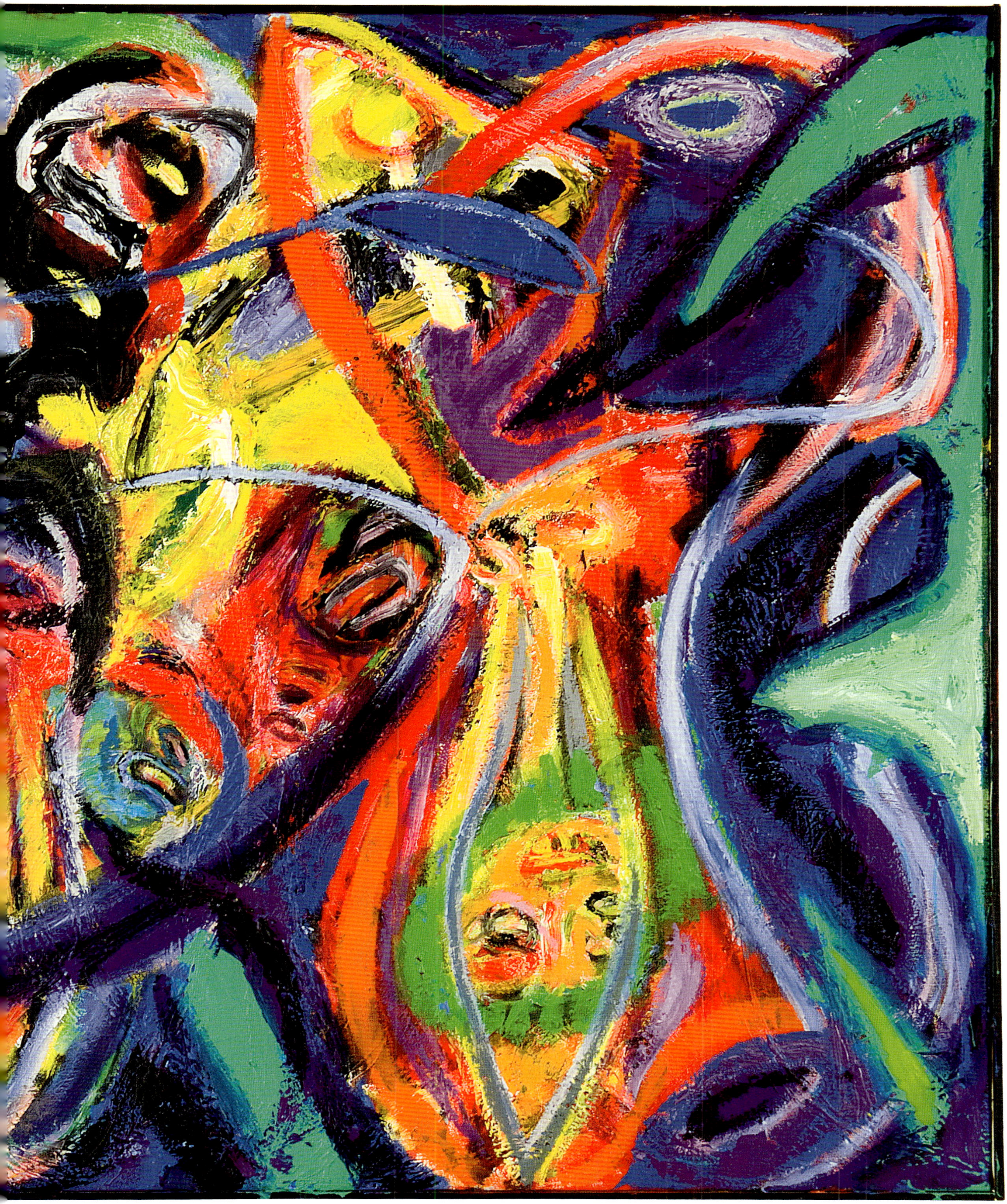

Sword and Serpent
Schwert und Schlange

1987/1991/2009
Acrylic on canvas / Acryl auf Leinwand
96 × 62 cm

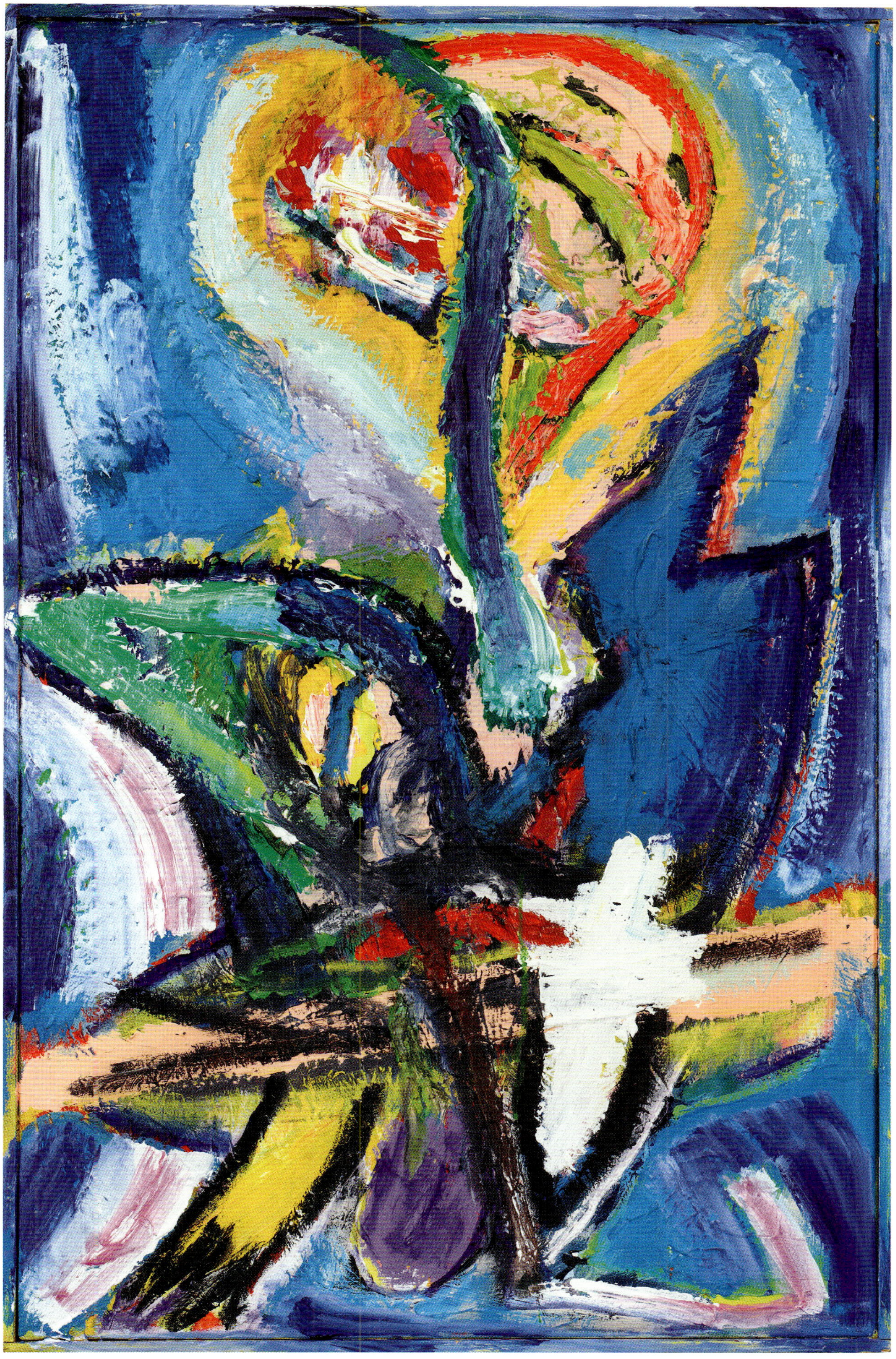

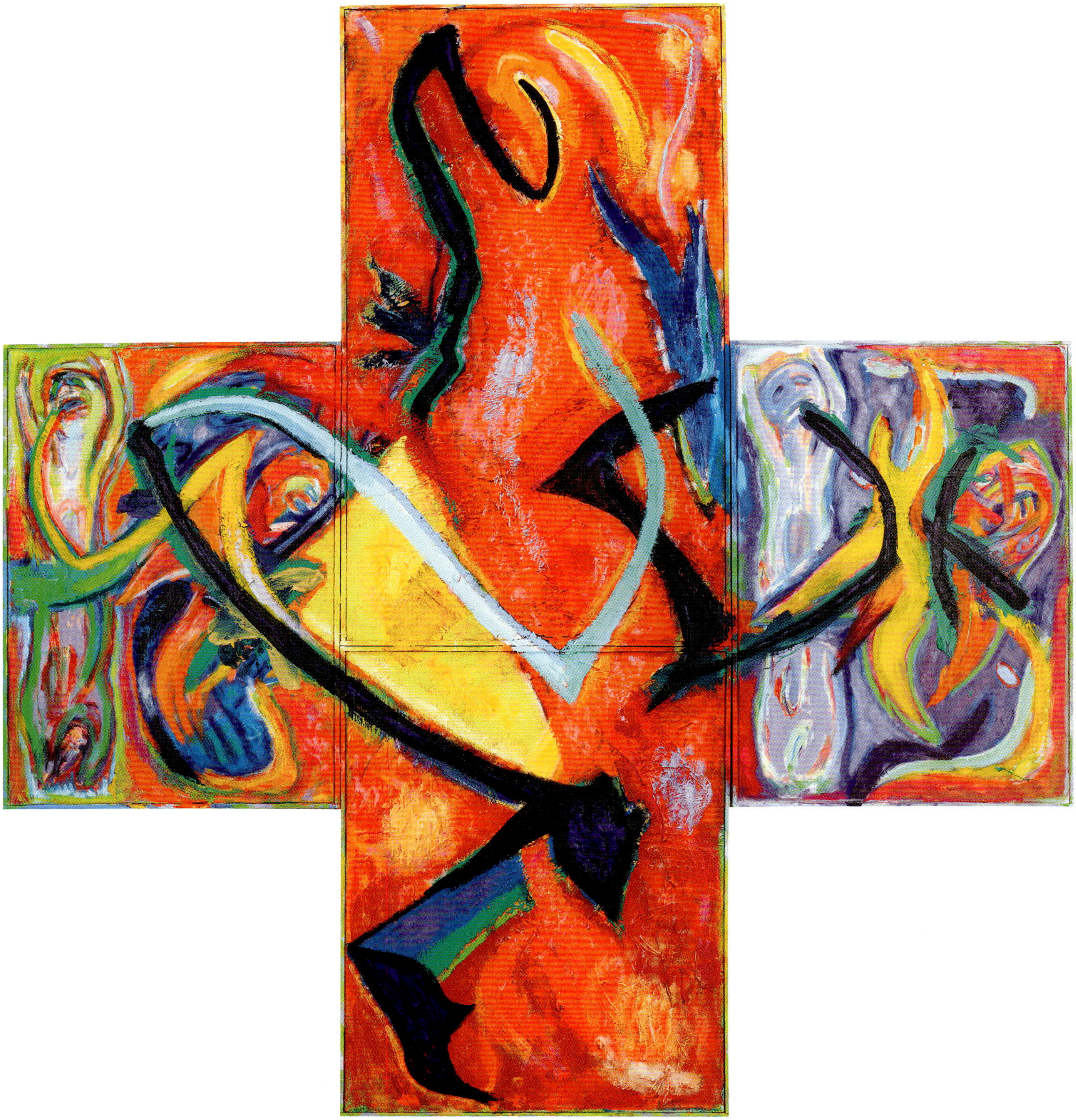

Space Cross
Raumkreuz

1989/1992/1993/2004/2008/2011/2012
Acrylic on four canvases, mounted / Acryl auf vier Leinwänden, montiert
244 × 227 cm

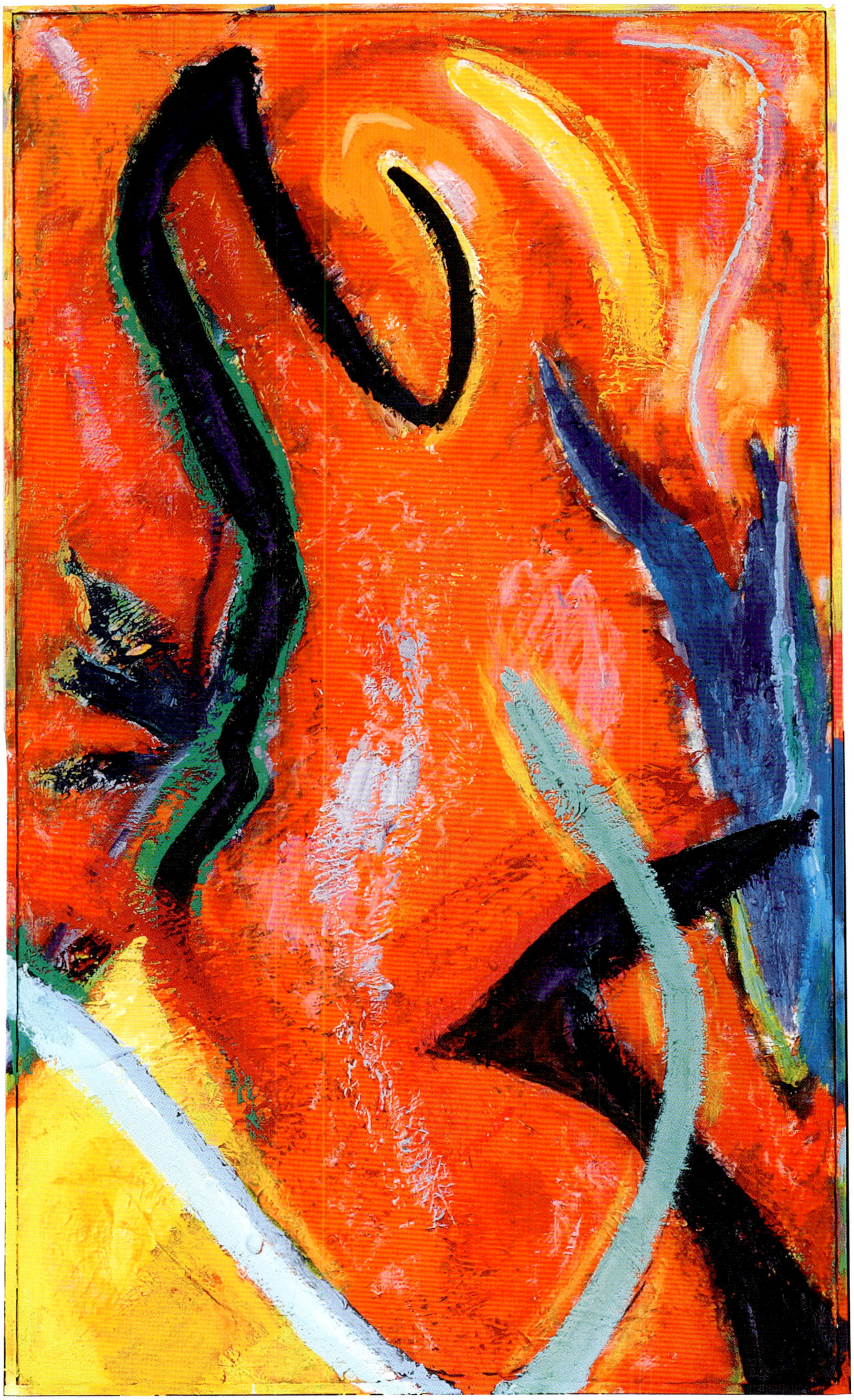

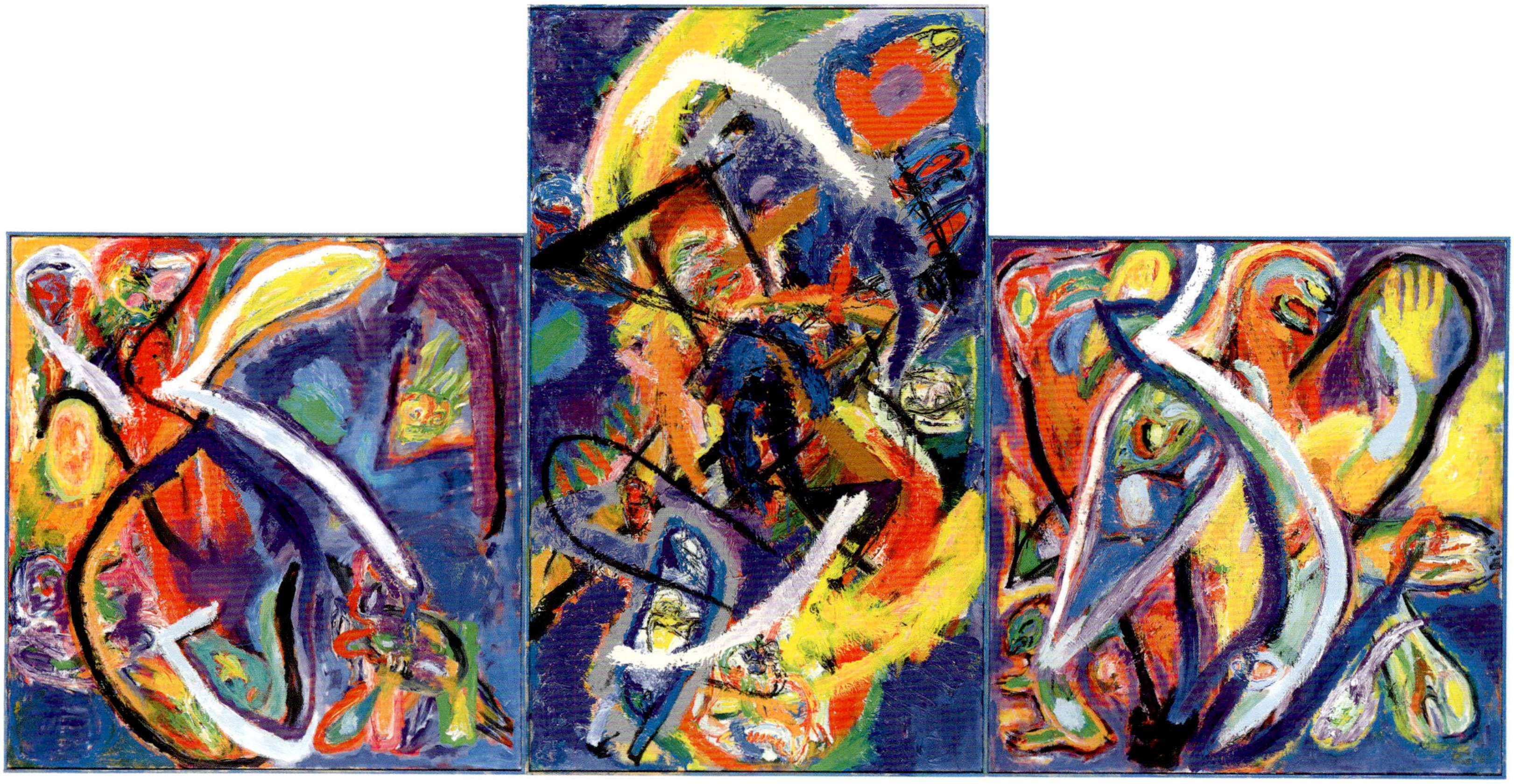

Chaos Cosmos
Chaos Kosmos

2006
Triptych, acrylic on three canvases / Triptychon, Acryl auf drei Leinwänden
202 × 380 cm

Kunsthalle Schweinfurt

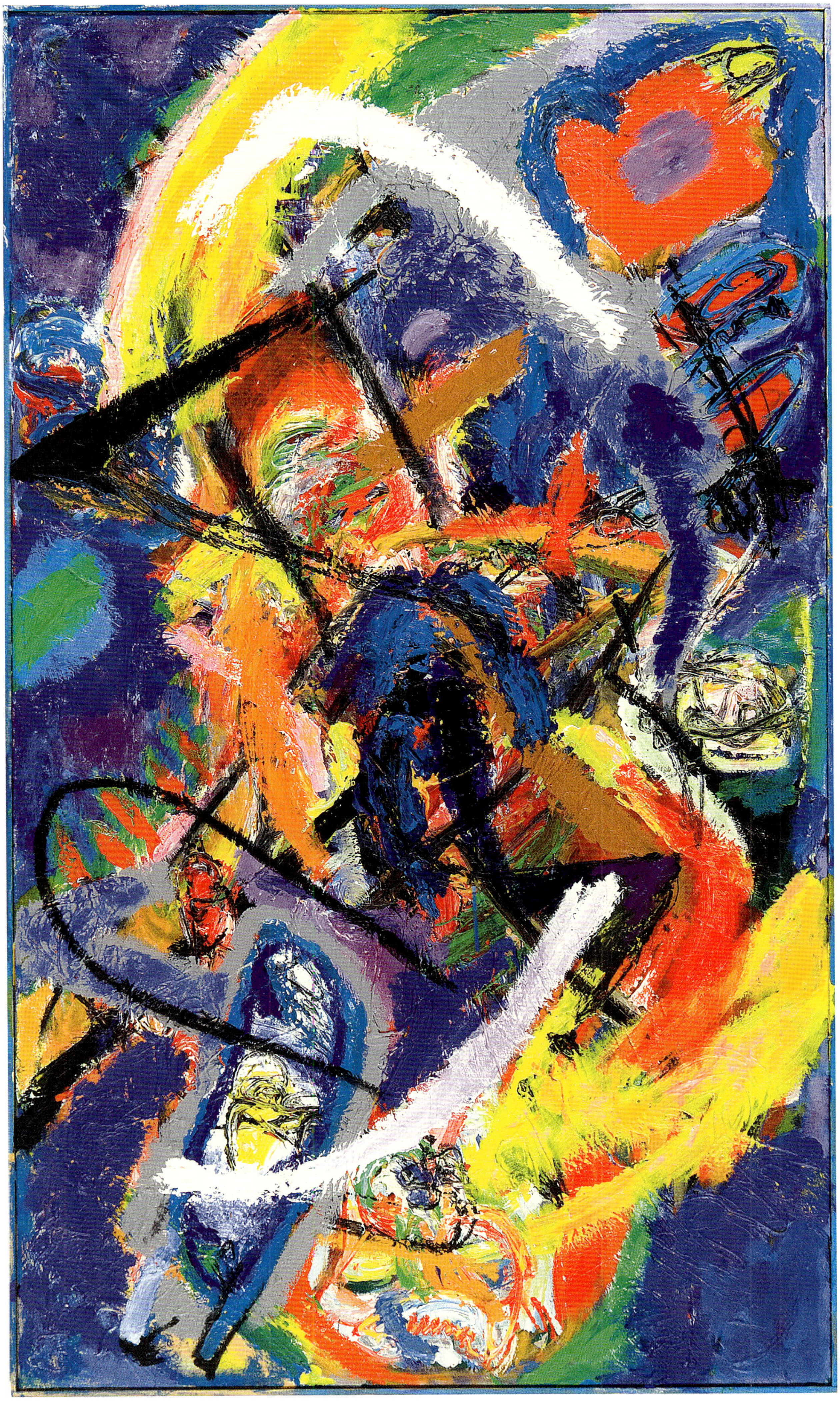

In the Red
Im Rot

2005/2011/2012
Acrylic on canvas / Acryl auf Leinwand
122 × 102 cm

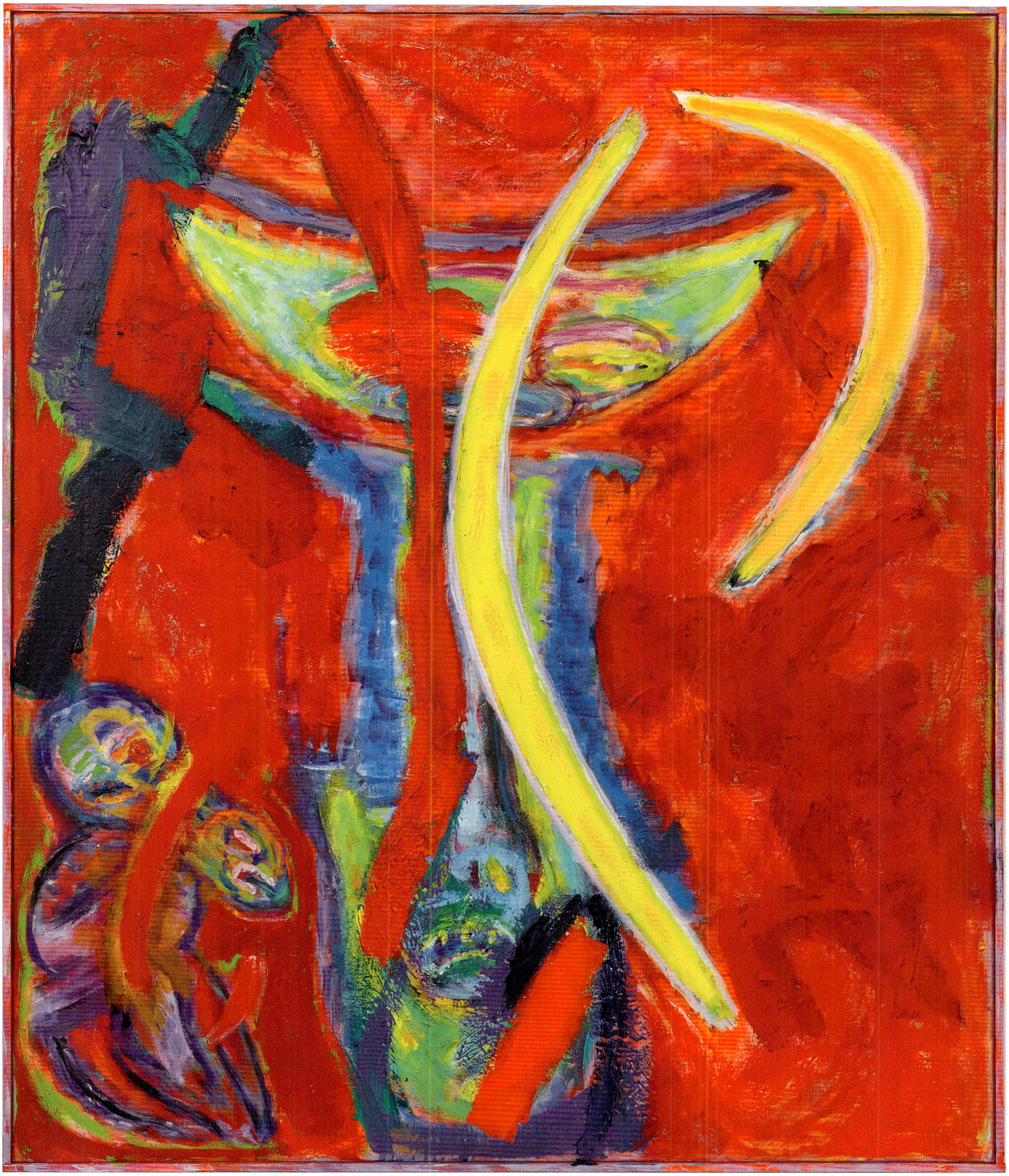

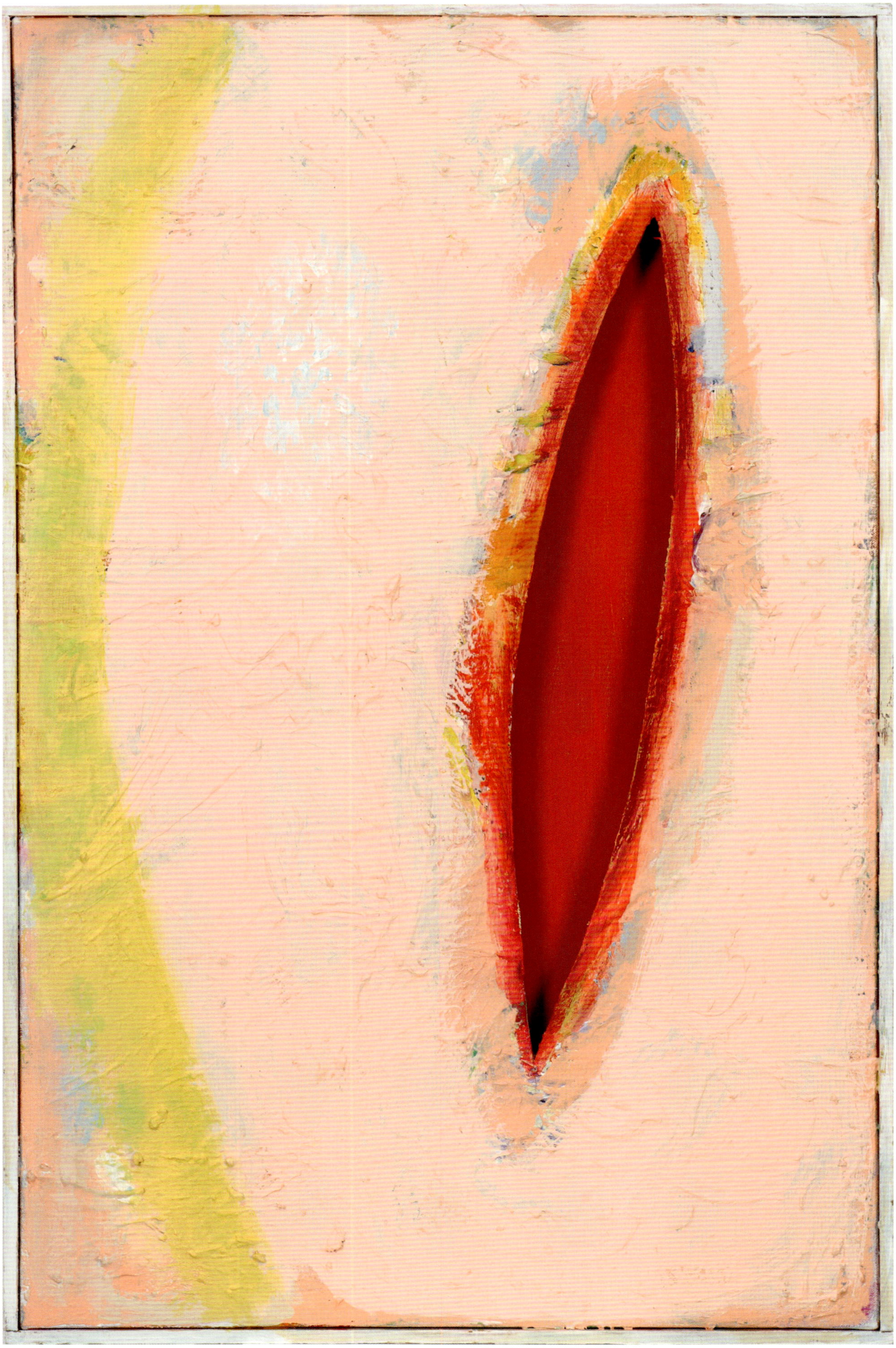

Slit Flesh
Spalt im Inkarnat

2000/2004/2009
Acrylic on canvas and wooden panel, mounted and cut / Acryl auf Leinwand und Holzplatte, montiert und geschnitten
98 × 62 cm

Slit Red
Spalt im Rot

2009/2011/2012
Acrylic on canvas / Acryl auf Leinwand
82 × 62 cm

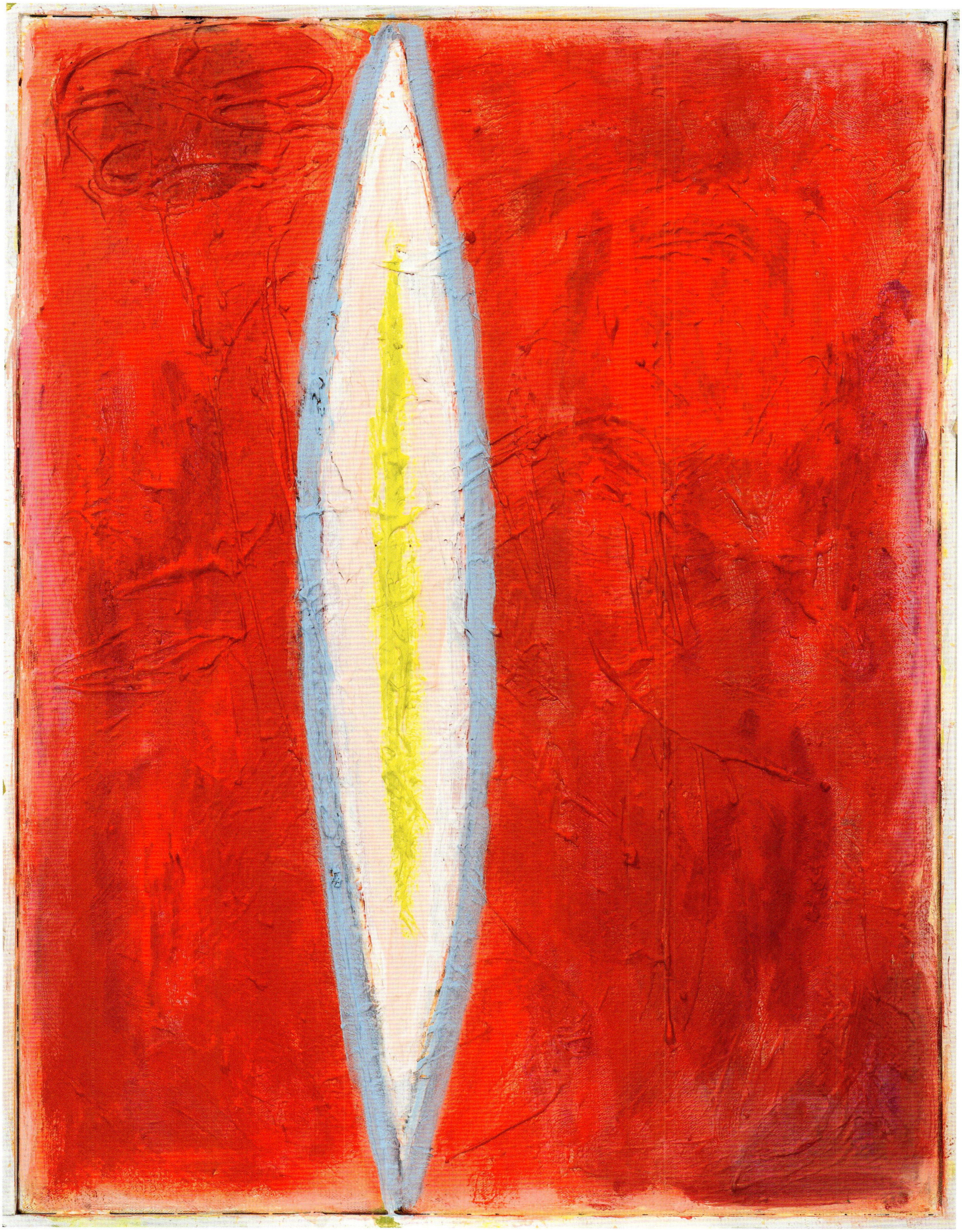

Sign
Zeichen

2012
Acrylic on canvas / Acryl auf Leinwand
120 × 100 cm

HRH Duke Franz of Bavaria Collection / Sammlung SKH Herzog Franz von Bayern

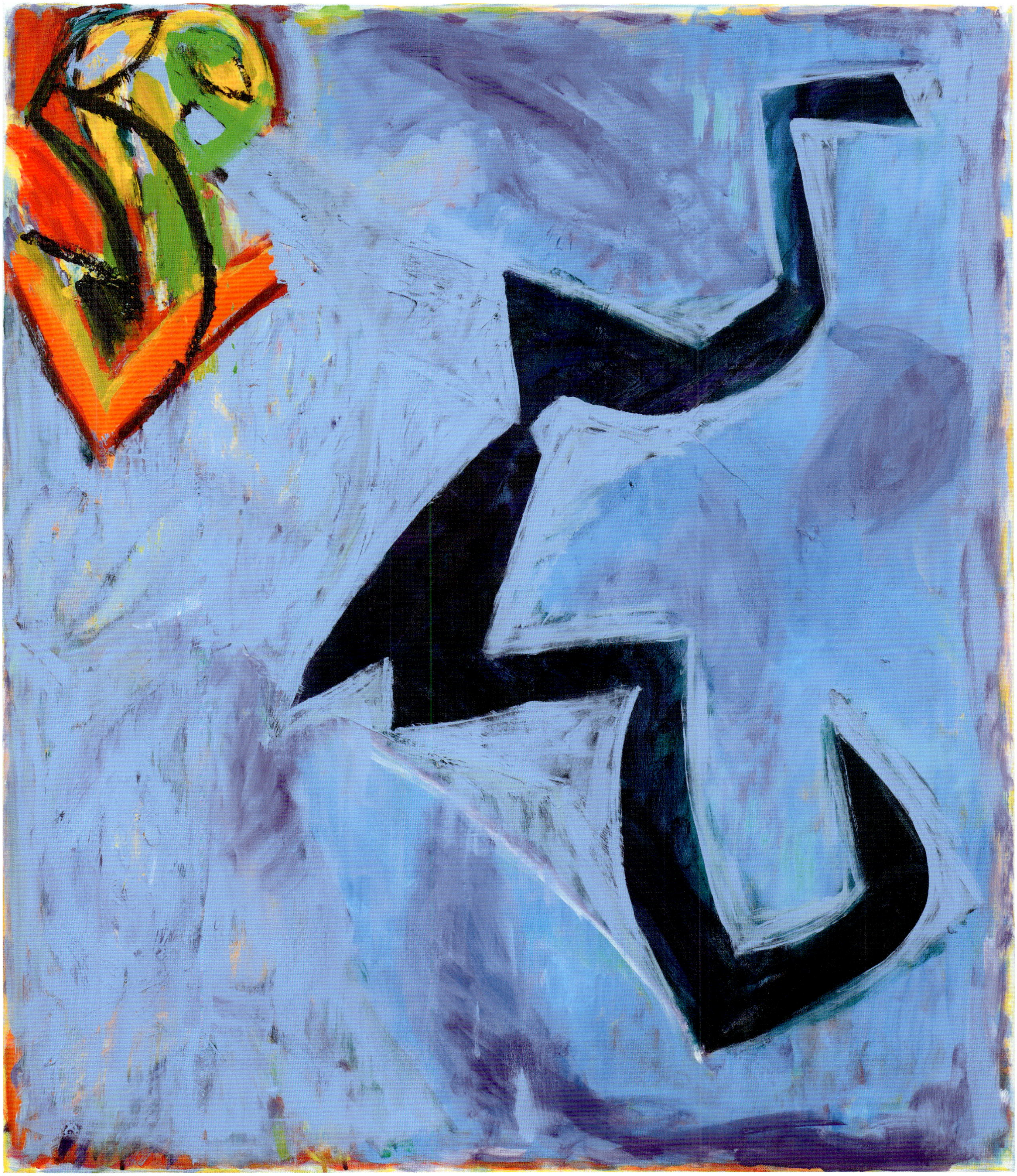

Highly Endangered
Äußerst bedroht

2012
Acrylic on canvas / Acryl auf Leinwand
120 × 100 cm

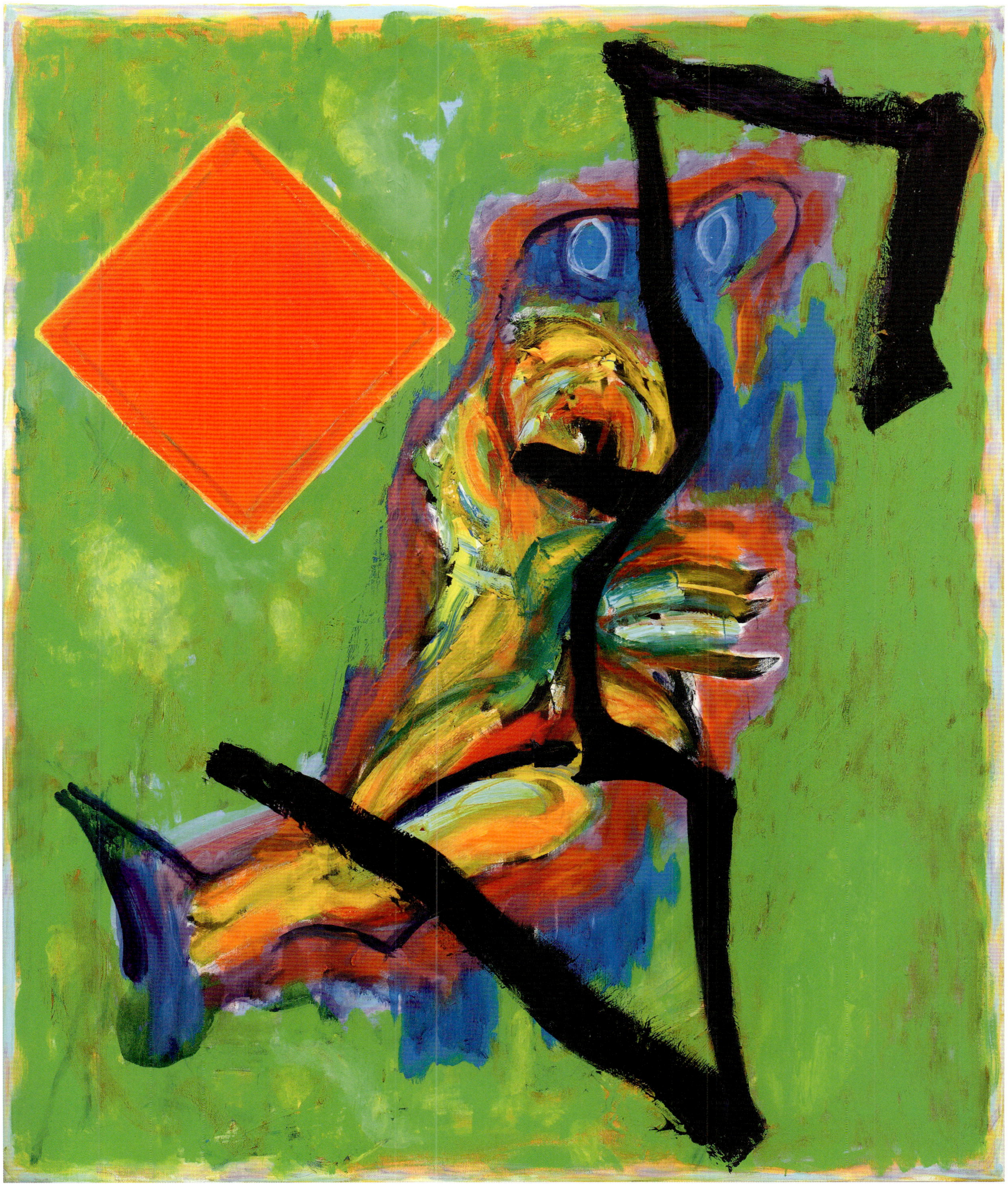

Death of Fear
Tod der Angst

2011
Acrylic on canvas / Acryl auf Leinwand
102 × 72 cm

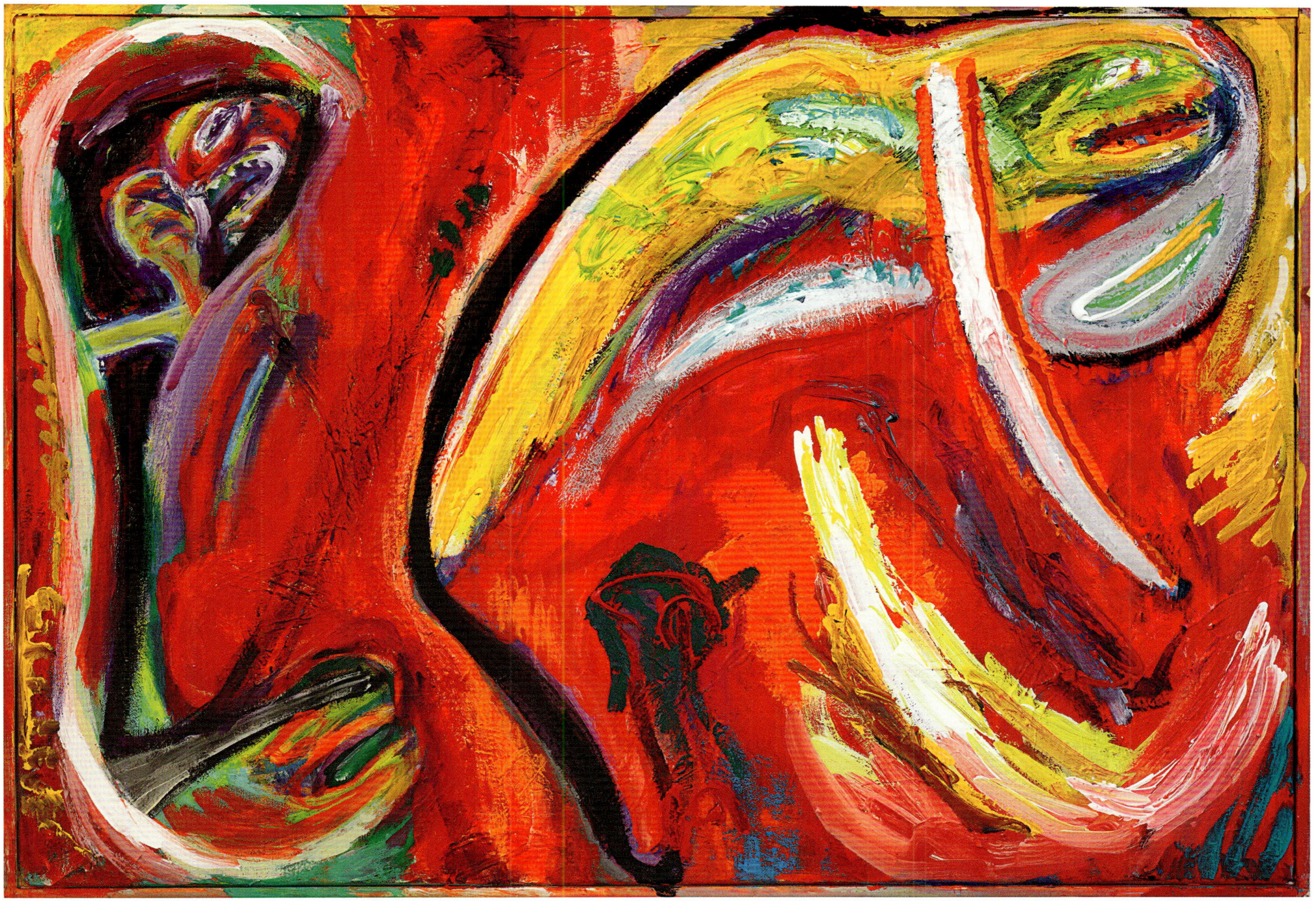

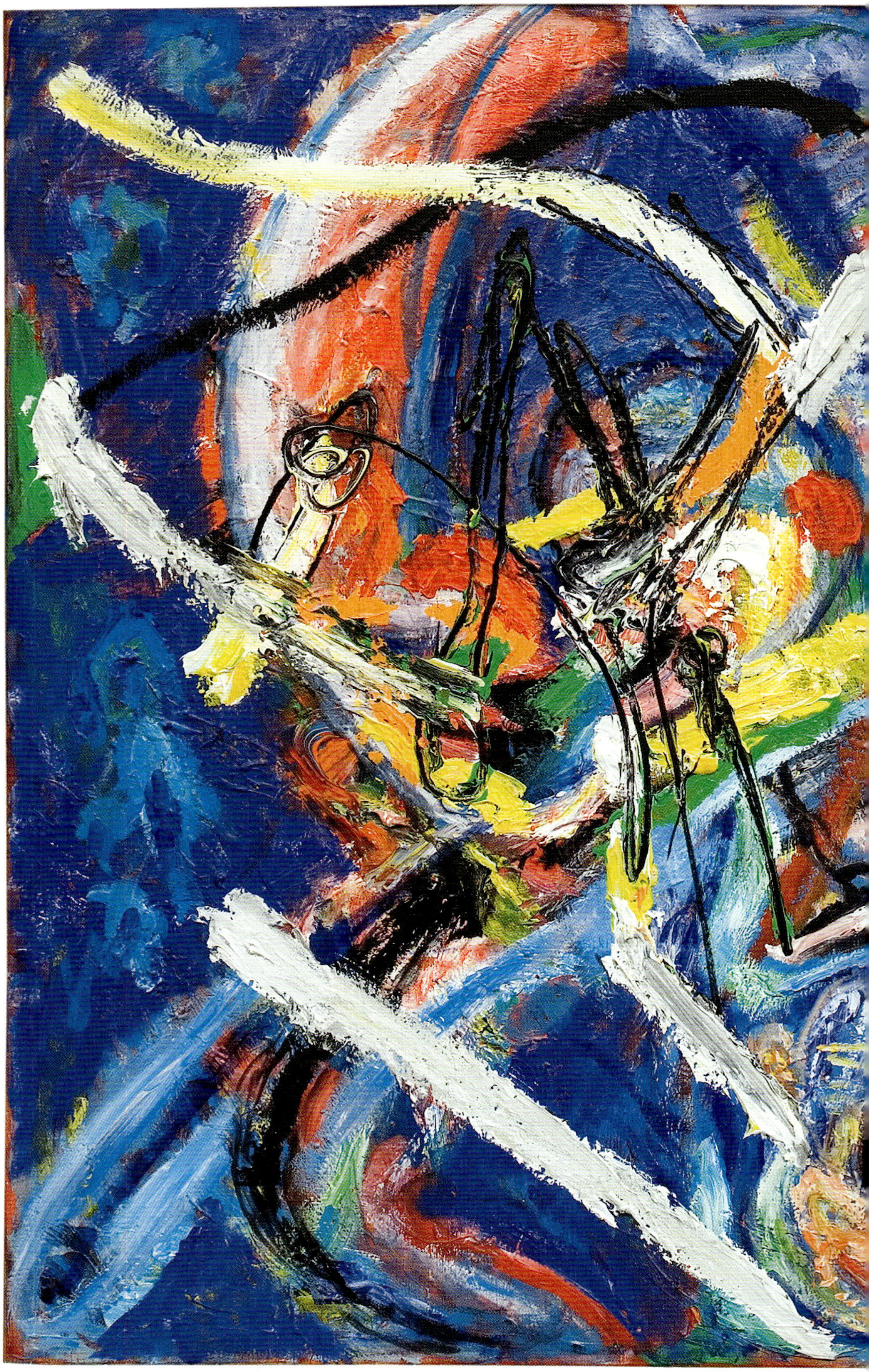

The River Came upon Me
Es betrat mich der Fluss

1998/1999/2005
Acrylic on canvas / Acryl auf Leinwand
140 × 221 cm

Schick Collection / Sammlung Schick

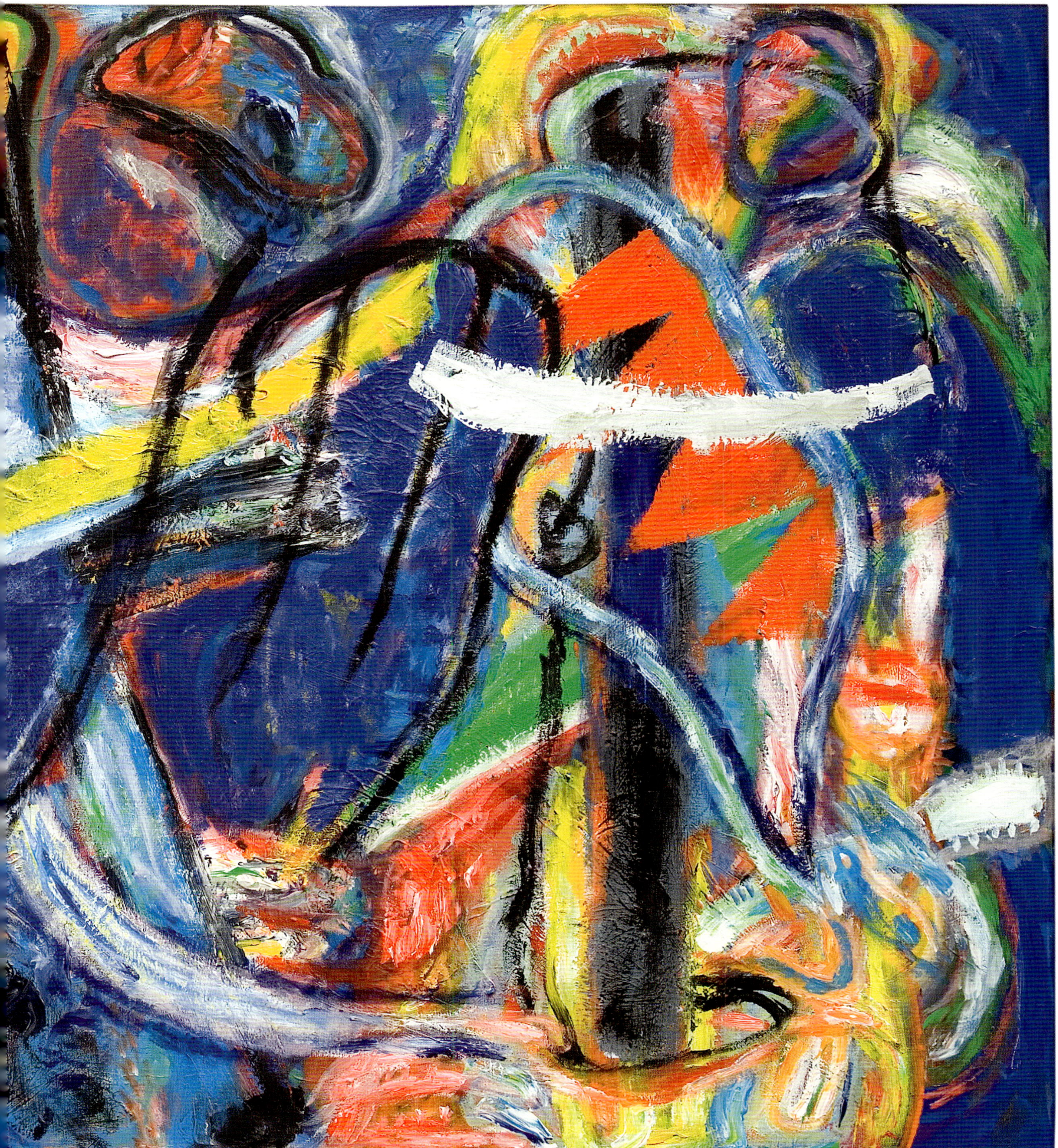

Encounter
Begegnung

2008
Acrylic on canvas / Acryl auf Leinwand
82 × 62 cm

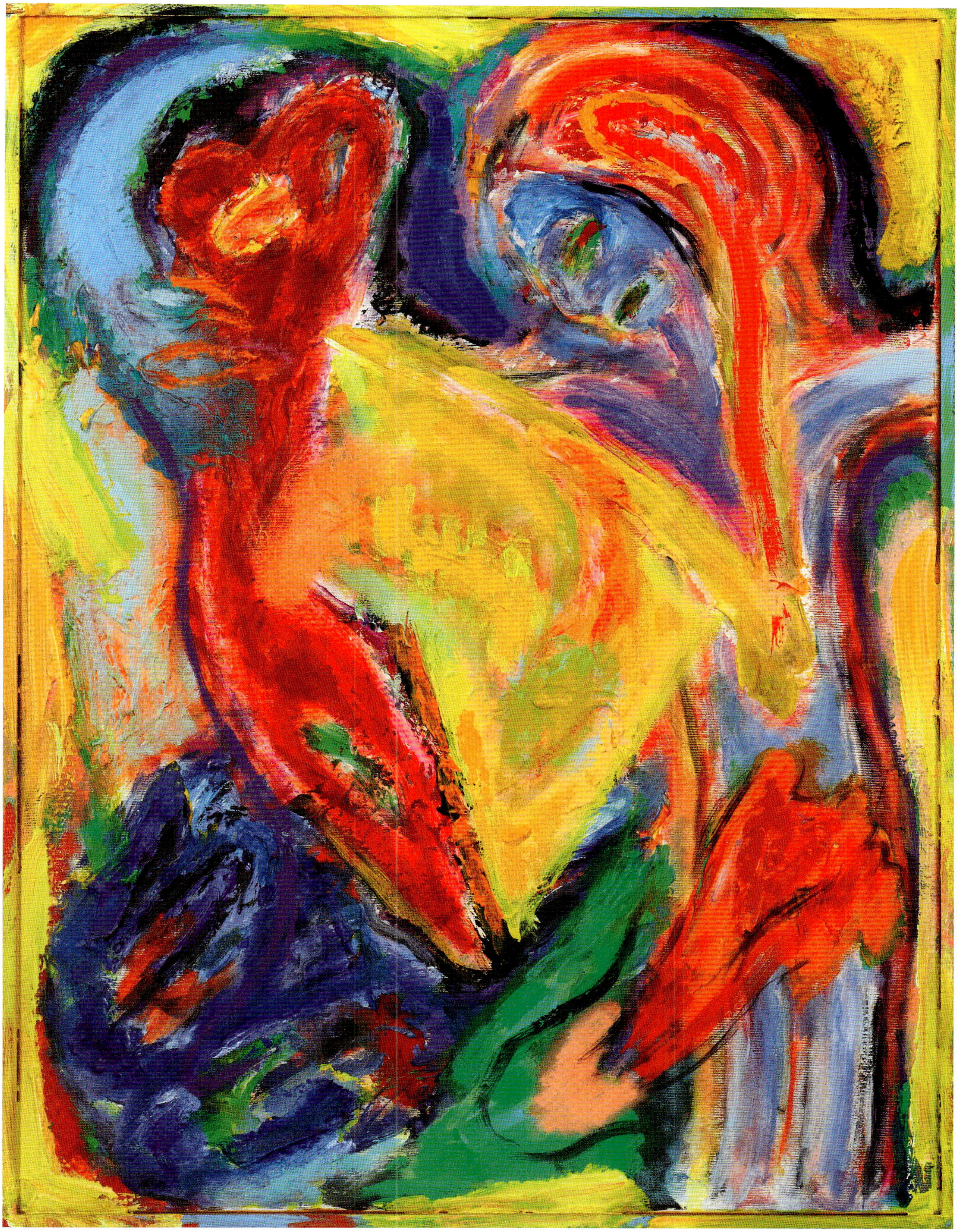

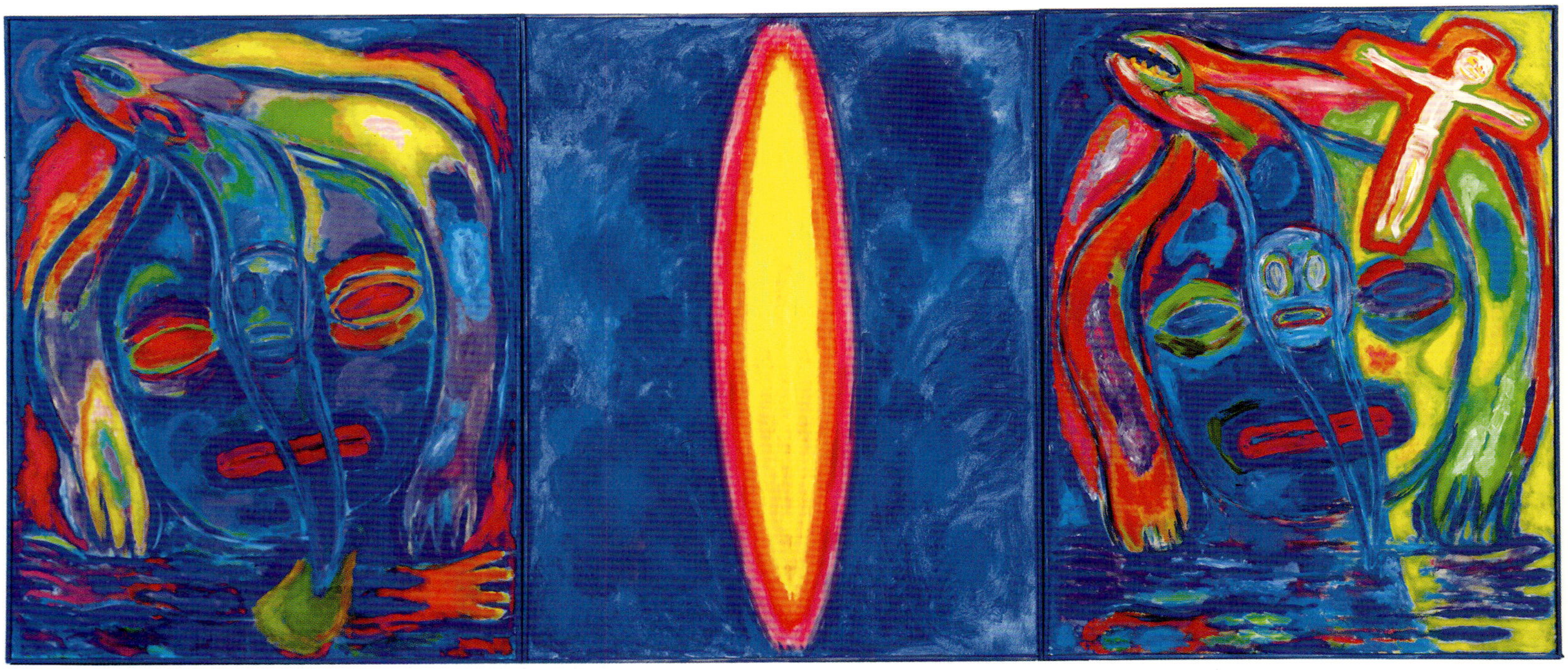

Meditation
Meditation

2001
Triptych, acrylic on canvas / Triptychon, Acryl auf Leinwand
170 × 390 cm

HRH Duke Franz of Bavaria Collection / Sammlung SKH Herzog Franz von Bayern

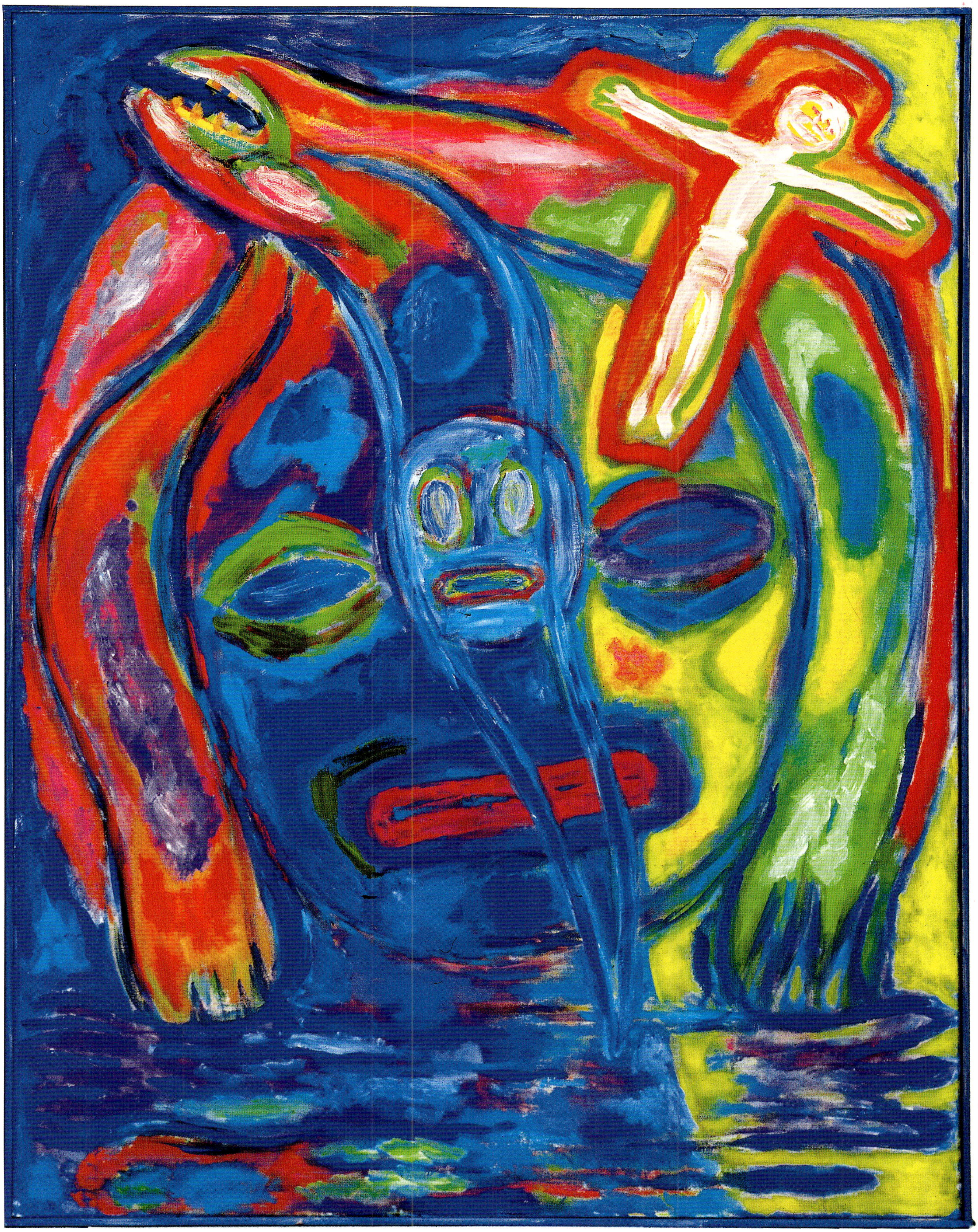

Countenance
Gesicht

2005
Acrylic on hardboard / Acryl auf Hartfaserplatte
90 × 60 cm

Galerie van de Loo Projekte

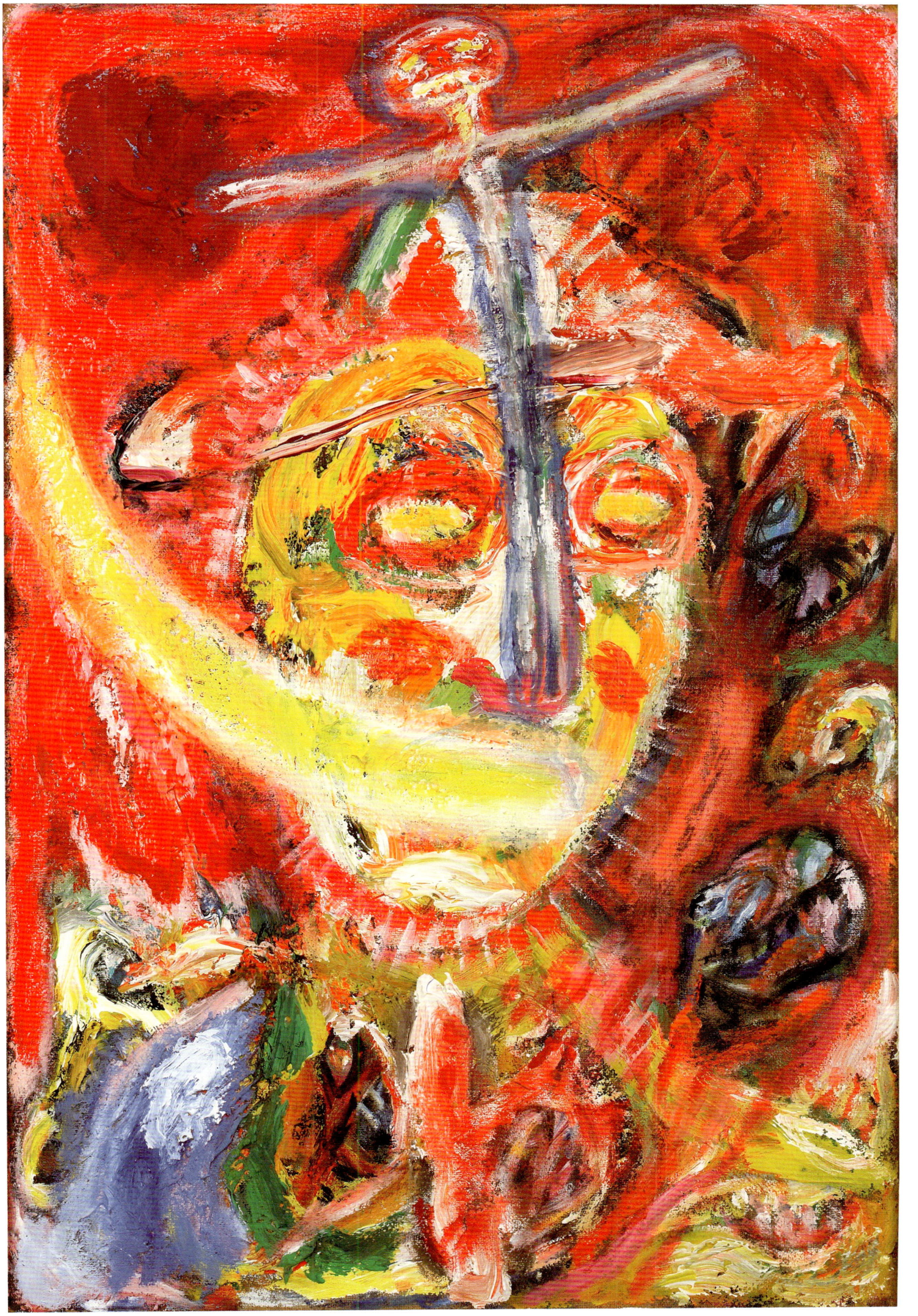

Fleeing Spirits
Fliehende Geister

2007
Acrylic on hardboard / Acryl auf Hartfaserplatte
72 × 102 cm

Kurt Schäfer Collection / Sammlung Kurt Schäfer

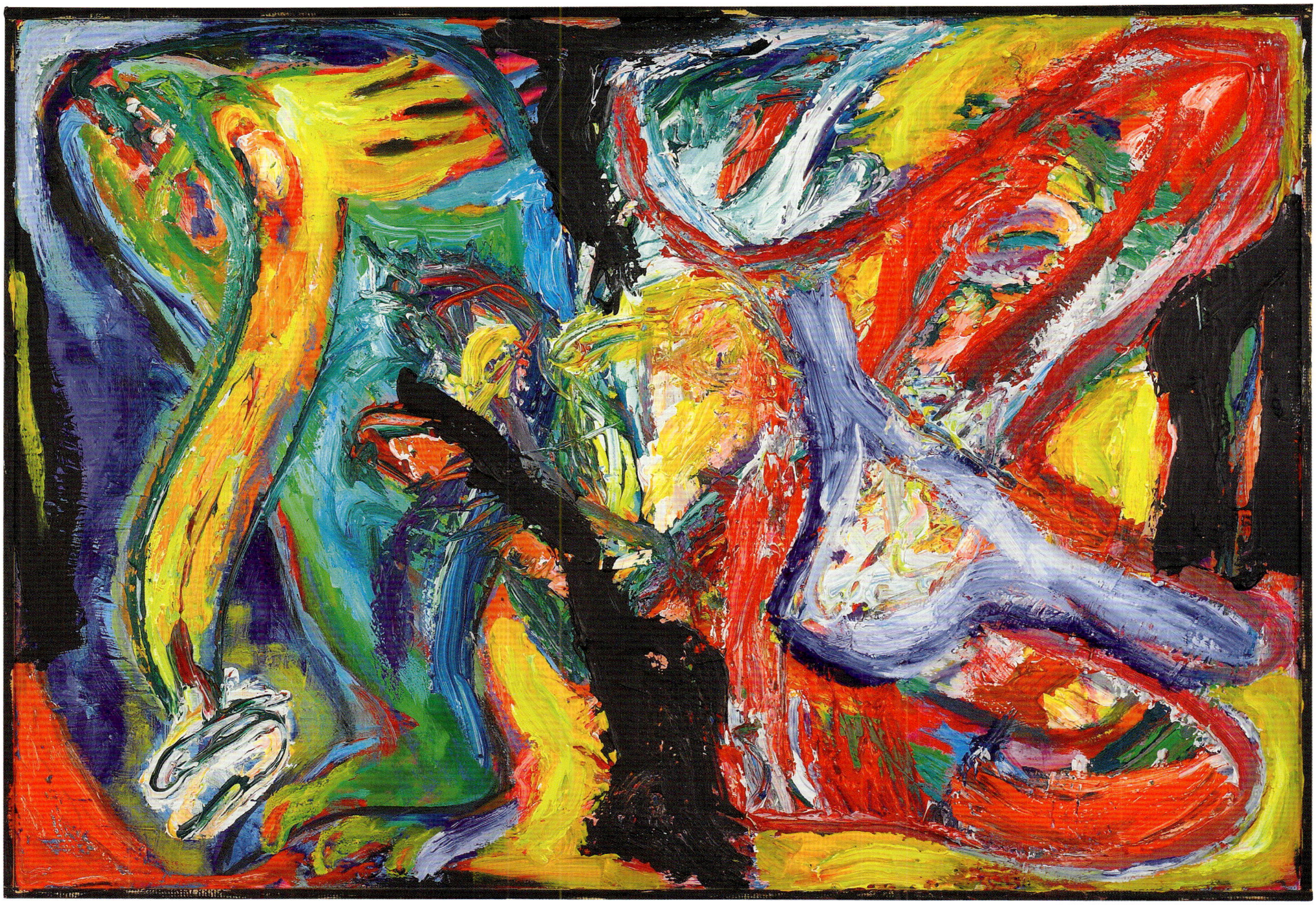

Oblivion
Raumvergessen

2011
Acrylic on canvas / Acryl auf Leinwand
100 × 70 cm

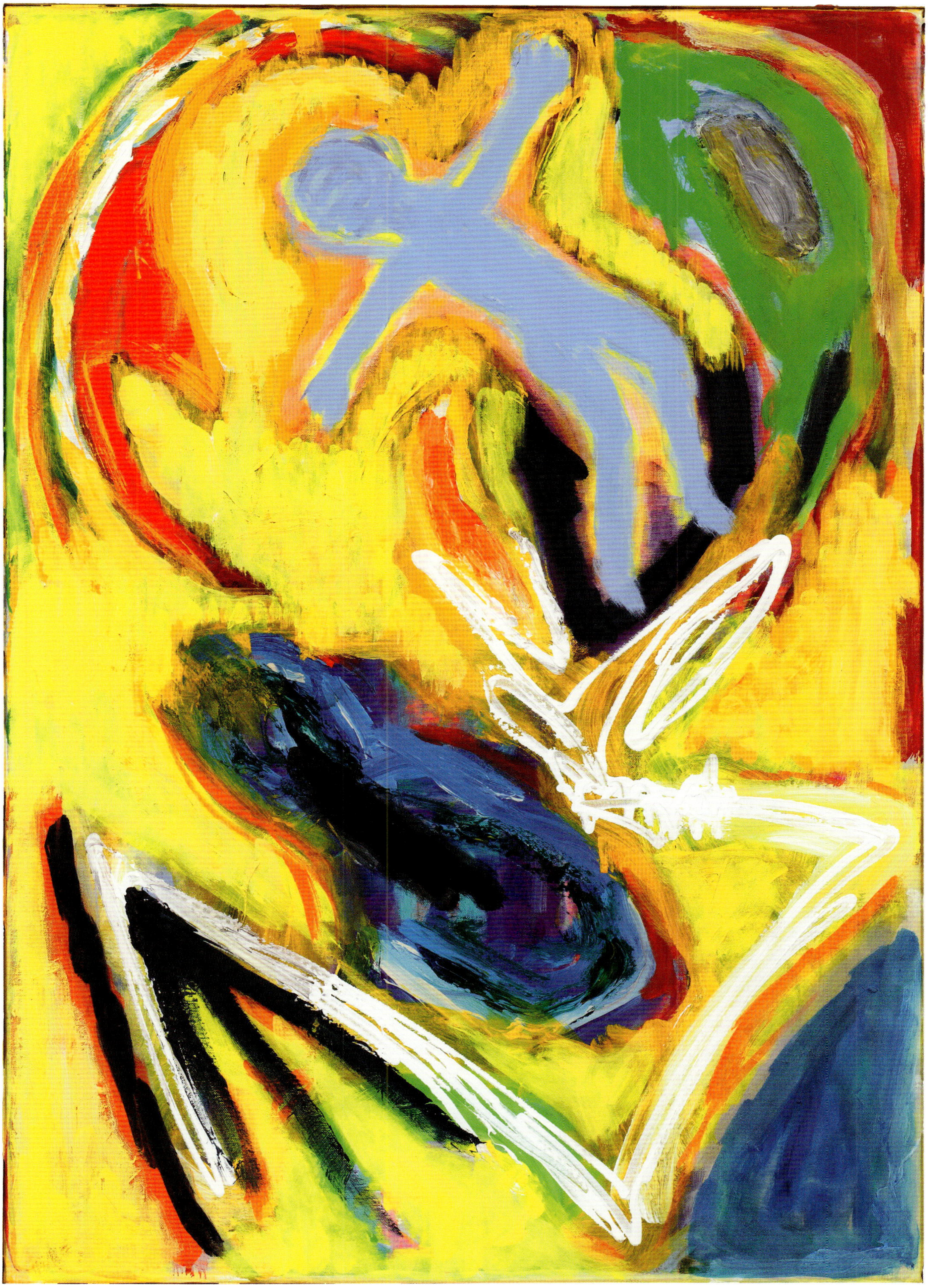

Inspired and Invisible
Seelenlicht und Schwarzgesicht

2003
Acrylic on canvas / Acryl auf Leinwand
102 × 72 cm

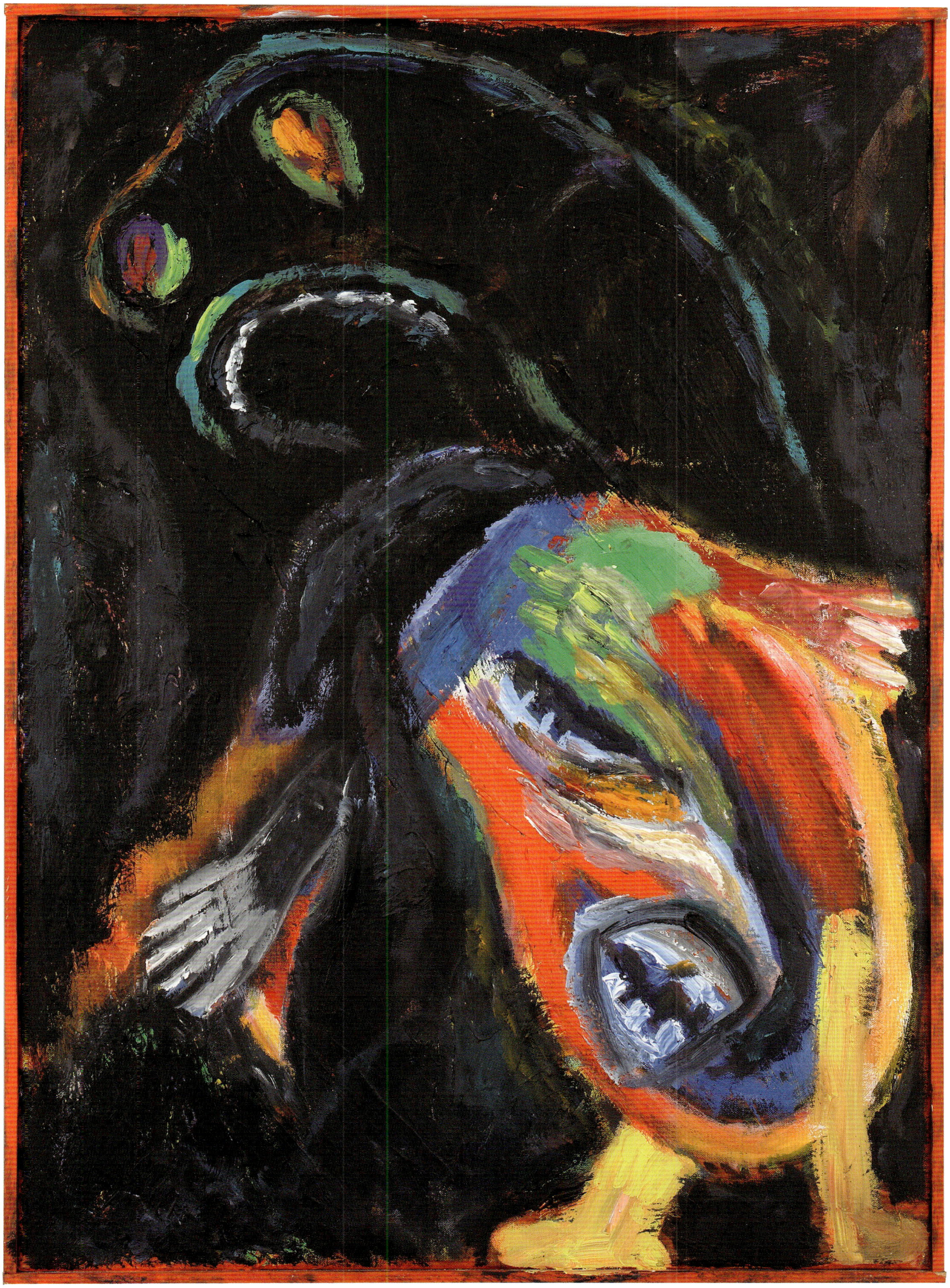

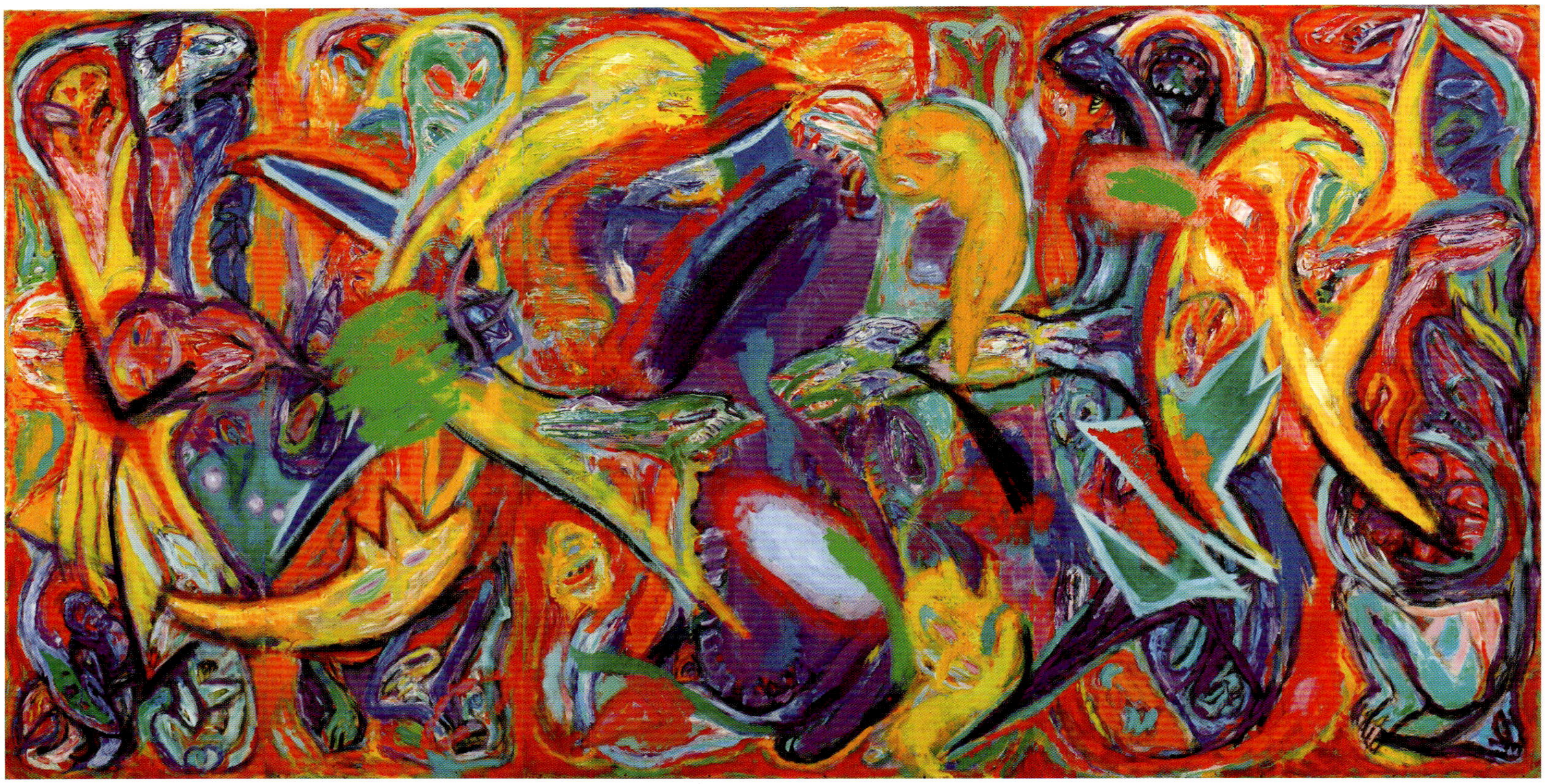

Memoirs of a Future Angel
Memoiren eines zukünftigen Engels

2006
Acrylic on hardboard (five sections) / Acryl auf Hartfaserplatten (5-teilig)
169 × 325.5 cm

DIE GALERIE, Frankfurt am Main

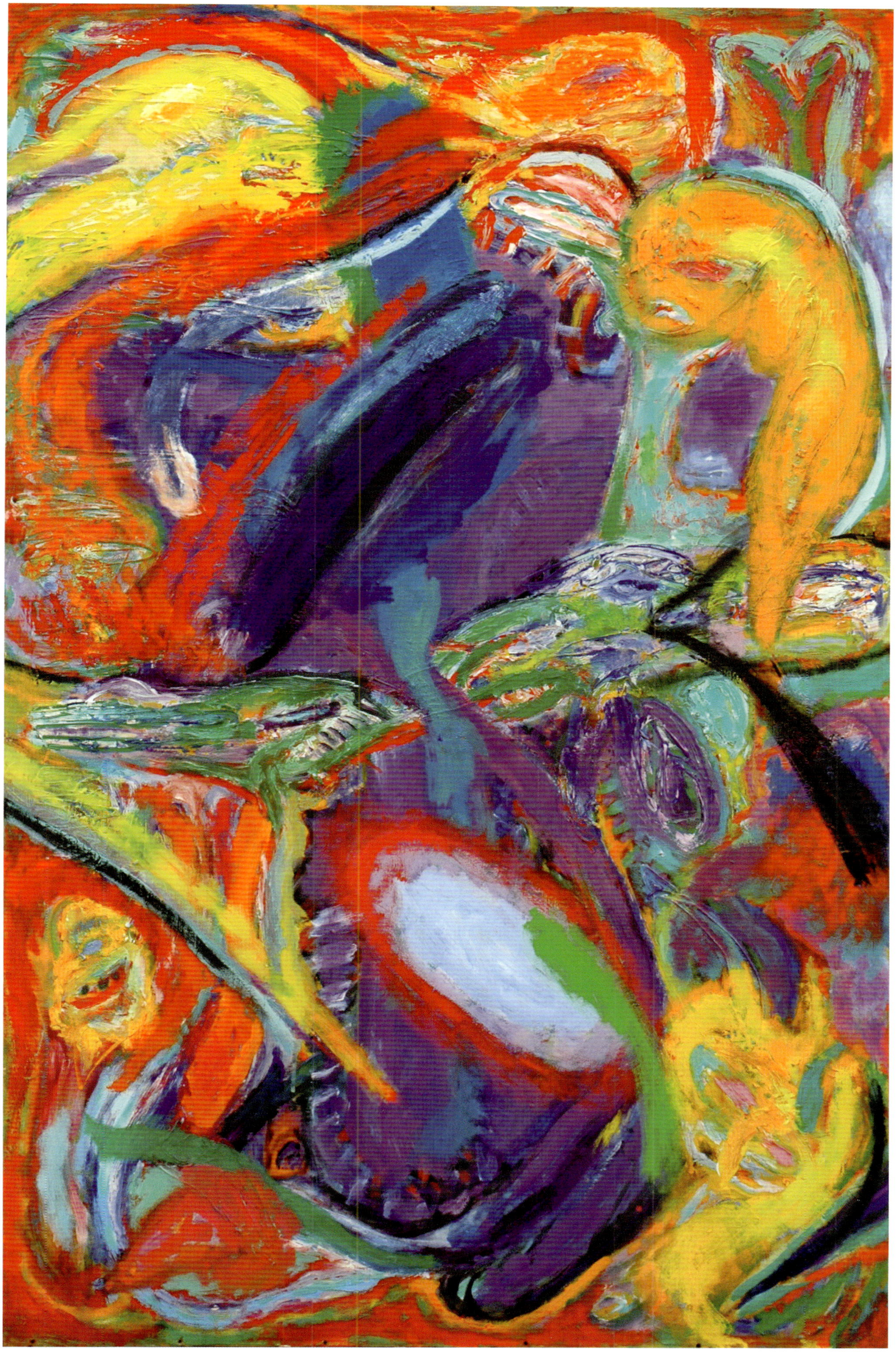

Scendere
Scendere

2003
Acrylic on canvas / Acryl auf Leinwand
70 × 60 cm

Marie-José van de Loo Collection / Sammlung Marie-José van de Loo

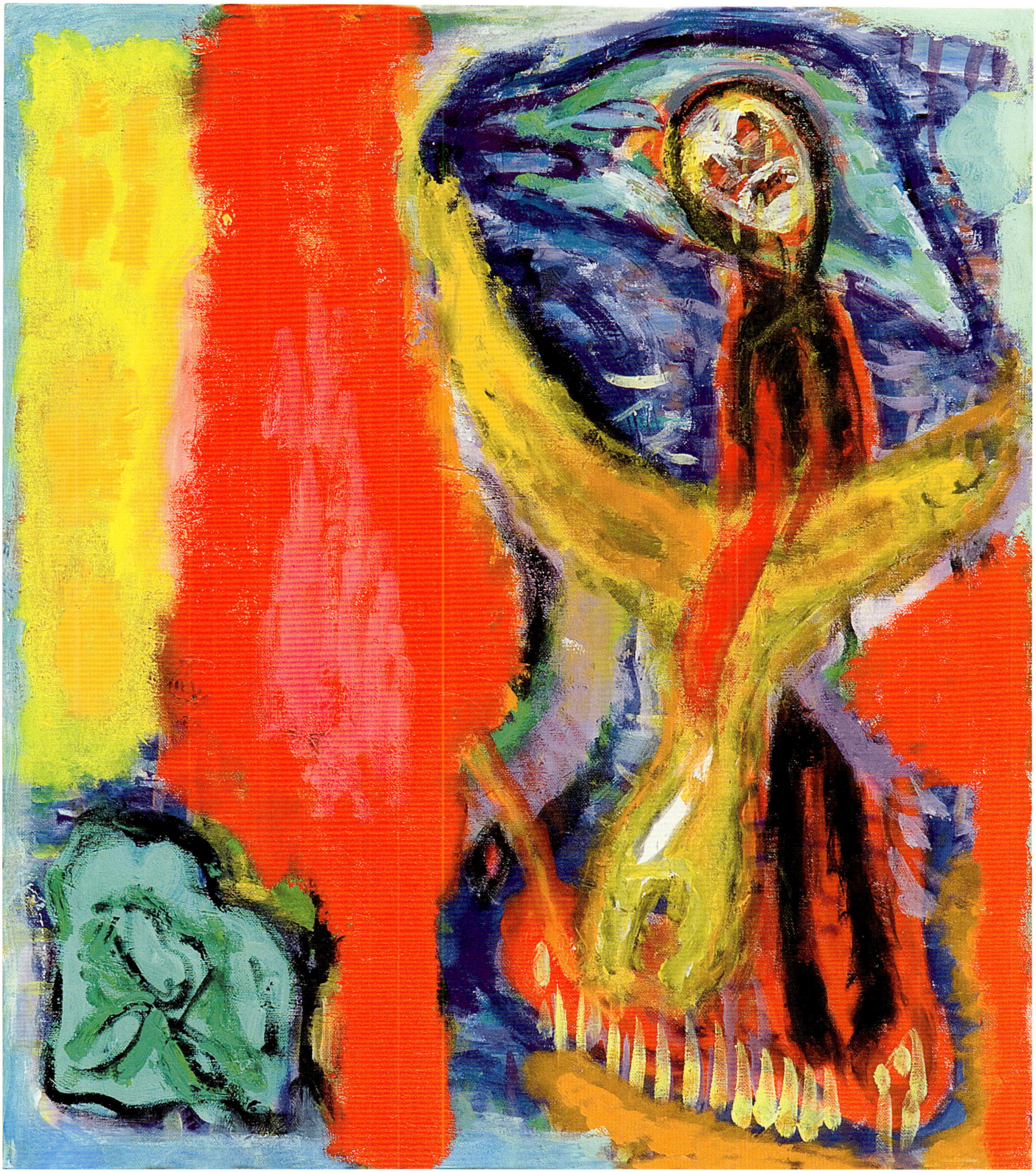

The Yardstick
Der Maßstab

2007
Acrylic on hardboard and lumber-core plywood, wooden batten, mounted /
Acryl auf Hartfaser- und Tischlerplatte, Holzleiste, montiert
133 × 133 cm

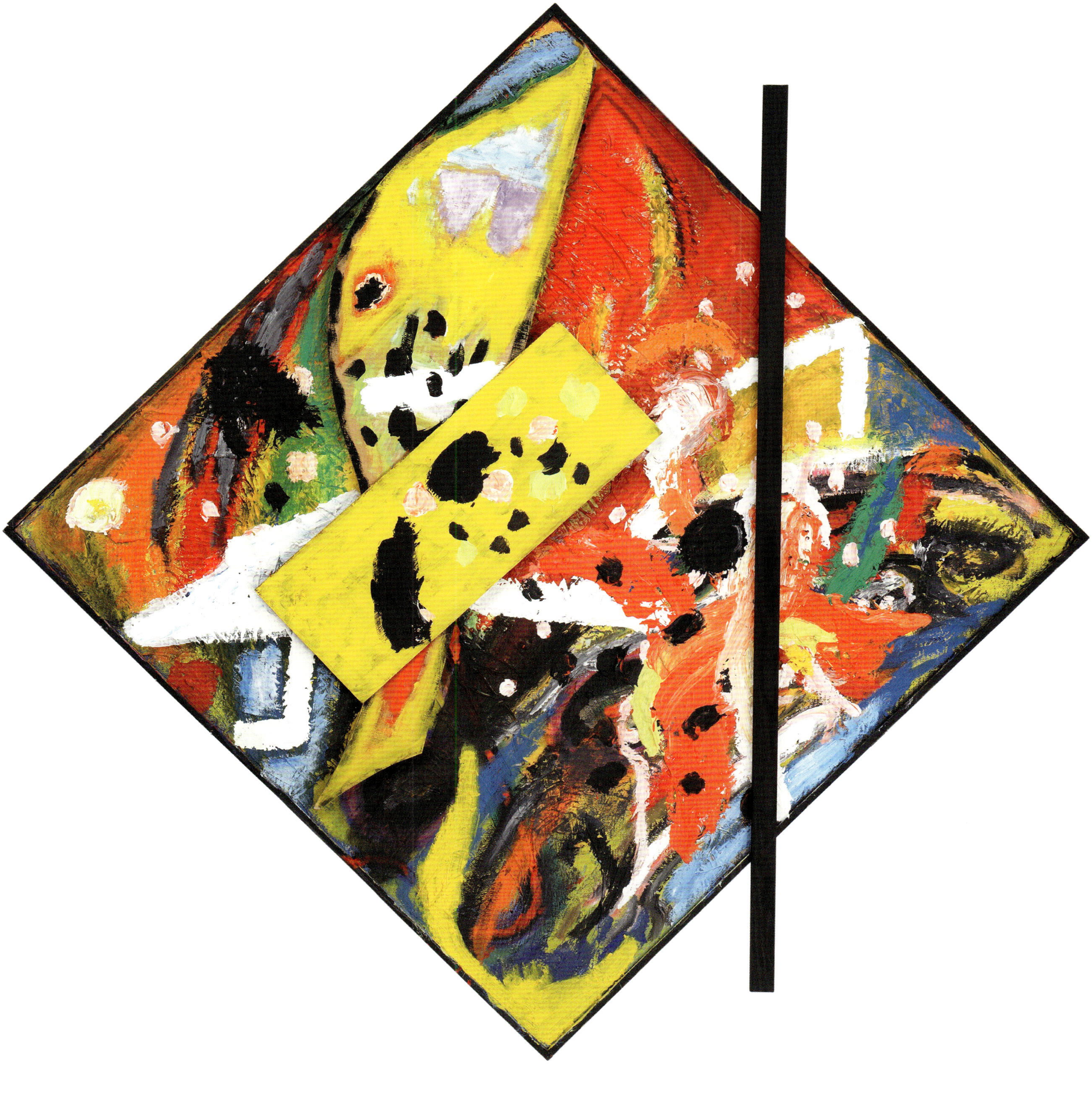

Toad's-Eye View
Die Sicht der Kröte

2007
Acrylic on hardboard / Acryl auf Hartfaserplatte
102 × 72 cm

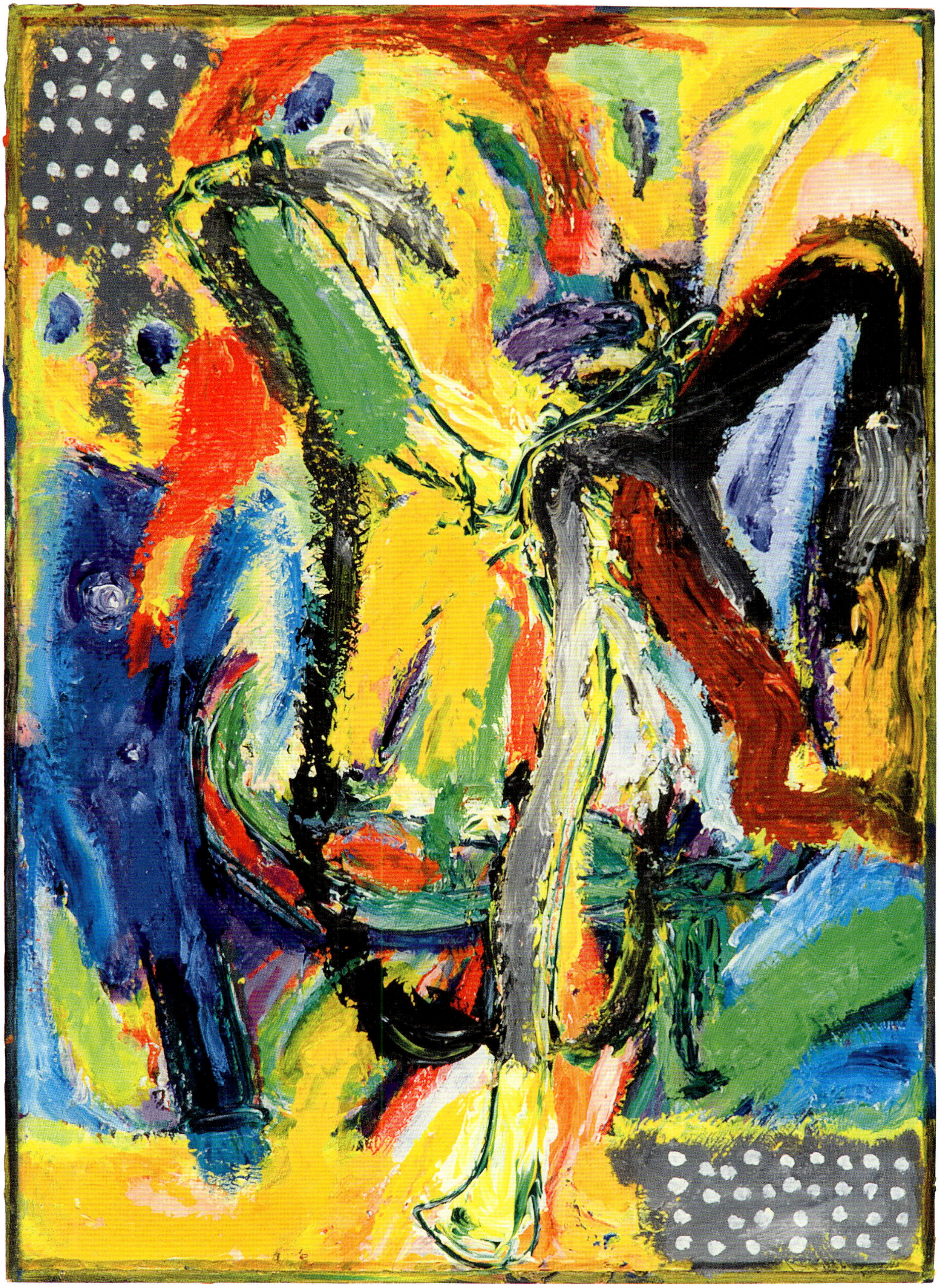

Portent
Menetekel

2002/2012
Acrylic on canvas / Acryl auf Leinwand
153 × 112 cm
Galerie Biedermann, München

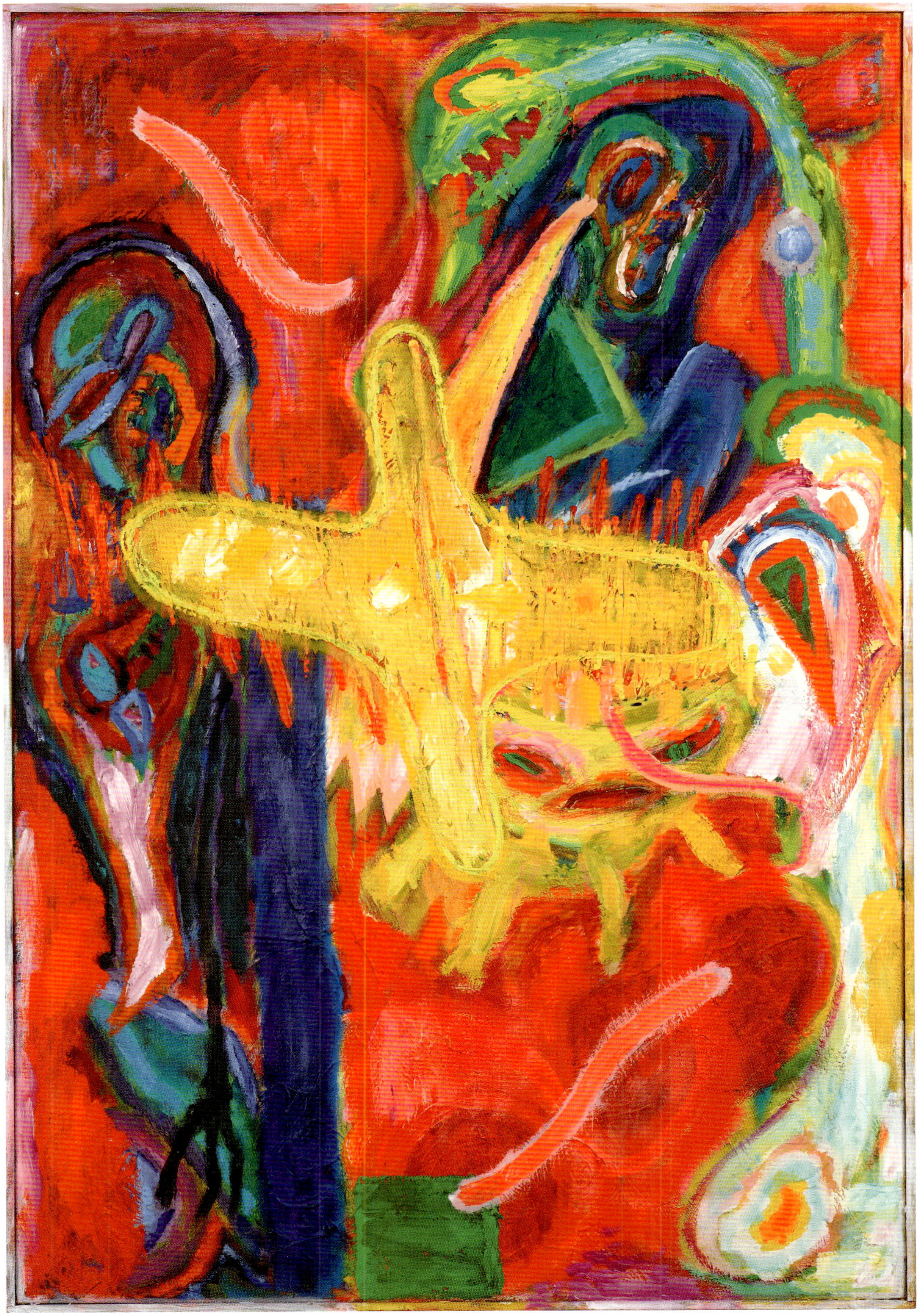

The fact that I became a painter is neither a coincidence nor fate.
It is rather a freely chosen mission.
I endure my life.
I form my pictures through pain and I create pictures in order
to rediscover what is real.
I open my eyes towards freedom.
It is so white that all the colours of the soul bow down.
Pain is dispelled by looking, and knowledge shapes our fate.
Colours are stars in the body of feeling. Like comets
they chase their brilliance into the picture and form the stream
from which I drink.
Painting is an action opened to the future.
It possesses the redeemed space.
It has the jubilance of being in becoming.
The dead will not die and the living will be released
in the ineffable.
We bear the shadow of the demon and reveal ourselves in the struggle for knowledge.
We are becoming, and no one knows the day when
we shall be.

Franz Hitzler

On the occasion of the presentation of the Friedrich Baur Prize
of the Bavarian Academy of Fine Arts, 2009

Dass ich Maler geworden bin, ist weder Zufall noch Schicksal.
Es ist vielmehr eine frei gewählte Mission.
Ich durchleide mein Leben.
Aus Schmerzen bilde ich meine Bilder und ich erfinde Bilder, um das Wirkliche wiederzufinden.
Ich öffne mein Schauen in die Freiheit.
Sie ist so weiß, dass sich alle Farben der Seele zuneigen.
Schmerz vergeht im Anschauen, und Erkennen bildet Schicksal.
Farben sind Sterne im Körper der Empfindung. Wie Kometen jagen sie ihr Leuchten ins Bild und formen den Strom, aus dem ich trinke.
Die Malerei ist eine in die Zukunft geöffnete Tat.
Sie hat den erlösten Raum.
Sie hat den Jubel des Seins im Werden.
Das Tote will nicht sterben und das Lebendige will erlöst sein im Unnennbaren.
Wir tragen den Schatten des Dämons und offenbaren uns im Ringen um Erkenntnis.
Wir sind im Werden, und keiner weiß um den Tag, an dem wir sind.

Franz Hitzler

Anlässlich der Verleihung des Friedrich-Baur-Preises
der Bayerischen Akademie der Schönen Künste, 2009

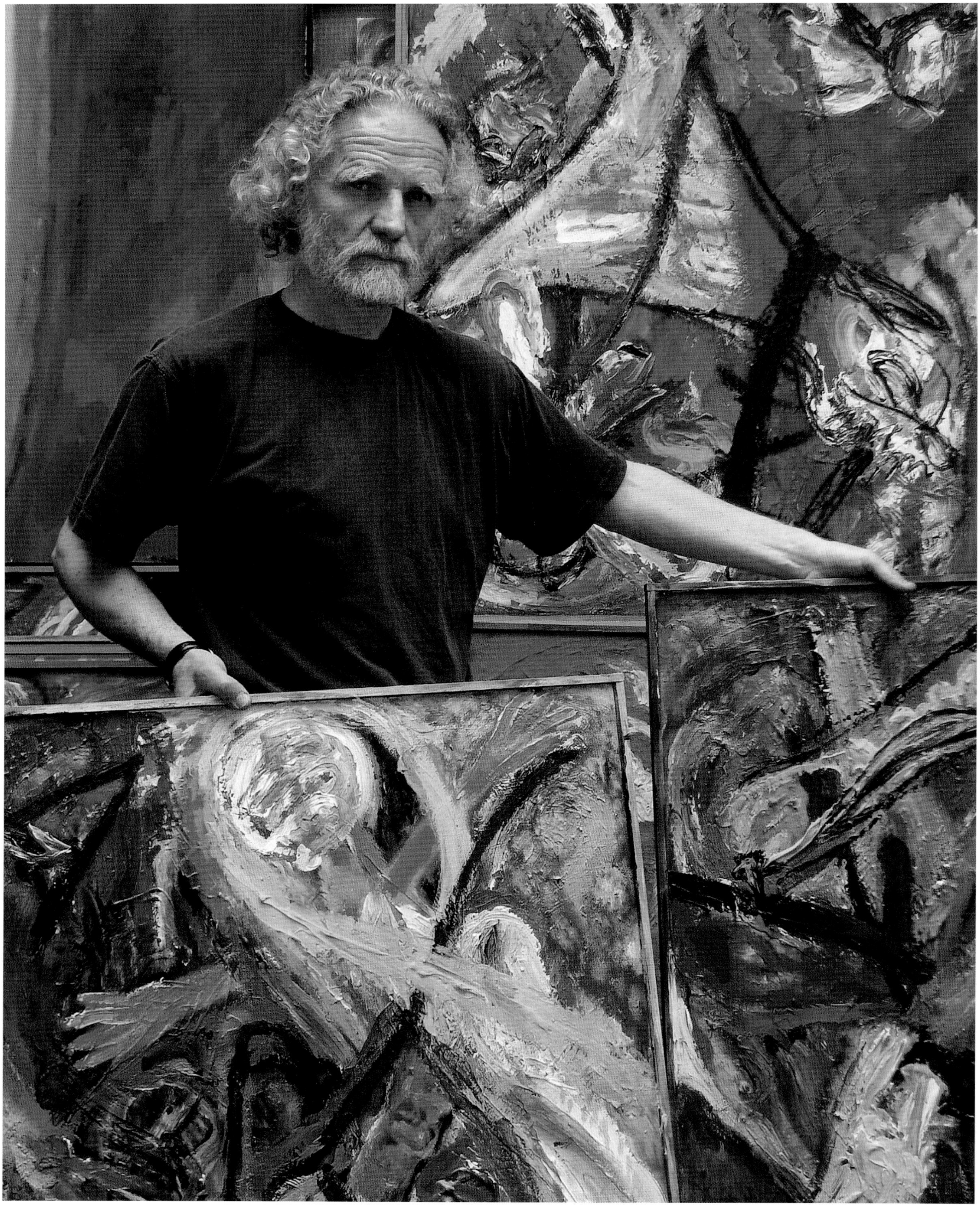

Biography

1946

born in Thalmassing bei Regensburg

1962–1964

College of Art, Augsburg

1967–1972

Academy of Fine Arts, Munich

1981

Bavarian State Prize for Art

Since 1997

Full Member of the Bavarian Academy of Fine Arts

Since 2002

Regular study visits to the San Giorgio ceramics studio in Albissola, Italy

2009

Friedrich Baur Prize of the Bavarian Academy of Fine Arts

2011

The Swabian region's Art Prize for his artistic œuvre

Franz Hitzler lives and works in Munich and the Allgäu region.

Biografie

1946

geboren in Thalmassing bei Regensburg

1962–1964

Werkkunstschule Augsburg

1967–1972

Akademie der Bildenden Künste München

1981

Bayerischer Staatsförderpreis Bildende Kunst

Seit 1997

Ordentliches Mitglied der Bayerischen Akademie der Schönen Künste

Seit 2002

regelmäßige Arbeitsaufenthalte in der Keramikwerkstatt „St. Giorgio" in Albissola, Italien

2009

Friedrich-Baur-Preis der Bayerischen Akademie der Schönen Künste

2011

Kunstpreis des Bezirks Schwaben für das künstlerische Gesamtwerk

Franz Hitzler lebt und arbeitet in München und im Allgäu.

Solo Exhibitions (a selection) / Einzelausstellungen (Auswahl)

1978

Galerie Heike Curtze, Düsseldorf/Wien

1979

Kunstforum Maximilianstraße/Altstadtring der Städtischen Galerie im Lenbachhaus, München. *Bilder 1977–1979 (Pictures 1977–1979)*

1980

Galerie Fred Jahn, München

Galerie Bloch, Innsbruck

Galerie Biedermann, München

Galerie Heike Curtze, Düsseldorf

Galerie Edeling, Kopenhagen

Kunstverein Bonn

1982

Galerie van de Loo, München, *Franz Hitzler 1976–1981*

Städtisches Museum Leverkusen, Schloß Morsbroich

Galerie Fred Jahn/Galerie Biedermann, München, *Skulpturen und Keramiken 1968–1982 (Sculptures and Ceramics 1968–1982)*

Galerie Academia, Salzburg

1983

Galerie Rudolf Zwirner, Köln

Galerie Thaddaeus J. Ropac, Lienz, Tirol

Galerie Edeling, Kopenhagen

1984

Galerie van de Loo, München

Galerie Fred Jahn, München

1985

Galerie Zwirner, Köln

Galerie Heike Curtze, Düsseldorf

1986

Galerie van de Loo, München, *Bilder 1985 (Pictures 1985)*

Galerie Fred Jahn, München

1986/87

Galerie-Verein München e.V.; Staatsgalerie Moderner Kunst, München, *Bilder 1975–1985 (Pictures 1975–1985)*

Städtisches Museum Leverkusen, Schloß Morsbroich

1988

Galerie Renate Kammer, Hamburg, *Arbeiten auf Papier (Works on Paper)*

Galerie van de Loo, München

1989

Staatliche Graphische Sammlung München, *Franz Hitzler – Druckgrafik (Franz Hitzler – Printed Graphic Works)*

Kunstverein Augsburg, *Bilder und Gouachen (Pictures and Gouaches)*

1990

Galerie Timm Gierig, Frankfurt am Main

Galerie Pospieszczyk, Regensburg

Kunstverein Reutlingen

Galerie Fahlbusch, Mannheim

Galerie Biedermann, München

Galerie Pels-Leusden, Villa Grisebach, Berlin

Galerie Fred Jahn, München

Galerie Rothe, Graphisches Kabinett im Westend, Frankfurt am Main

1991

Galerie Zwirner, Köln

Verein für Original-Radierung München e.V.

1992

Galerie Biedermann, München

Galerie Fahlbusch, Mannheim

Galerie im Schloß Haigerloch

1993

Museum der bildenden Künste Leipzig, *Franz Hitzler – Gemälde und Radierungen (Franz Hitzler – Paintings and Etchings)*

Galerie Fred Jahn, München, *Bilder der 70er Jahre (Pictures from the Seventies)*

Galerie Gunar Barthel, Berlin

1994

Graphisches Kabinett im Westend Dr. W. Rothe, Frankfurt am Main

Atelier-Galerie Oberländer, Augsburg, *Bilder – Zeichnungen – Radierungen (Pictures – Drawings – Etchings)*

1995

Galerie Rothe, Frankfurt am Main, *Farbige Skulpturen und neue Bilder (Coloured Sculptures and New Pictures)*

Galerie Biedermann, München

Galerie Kurt Schäfer, Berlin, *Gesichte (Vision)*

Forum Guardini, Guardini Siftung e.V., Berlin, *Franz Hitzler in St. Matthäus (Franz Hitzler in St Matthew's Church)* Kirchenraumgestaltung (Church interior design)

1996

Galerie Diehl & Partner, Silvaplana, Schweiz

Galerie Kurt Schäfer, Berlin

Galerie Fred Jahn, München, *Bilder, Zeichnungen, Skulpturen (Pictures, Drawings, Sculptures)*

Galerie Josephski-Neukum, Issing

Galerie Brigitte Ihsen, Köln

1998

Galerie Oberländer, Augsburg

1999

Galerie Biedermann, München, *Landschaften (Landscapes)*

Graphisches Kabinett Dr. Rothe, Frankfurt am Main, *Arbeiten auf Papier aus den 90er Jahren (Works on Paper from the Nineties)*

Galerie Titan, Frankfurt am Main

Galerie Fred Jahn, München

2000

Galerie Fred Jahn, München, *Zeichnungen 1998/99 (Drawings 1998/99)*

2001

Rathausgalerie der Landeshauptstadt München, *Metamorphosen (Metamorphoses)*, Ausstellung mit H. M. Bachmayer (Exhibition with H. M. Bachmayer)

Galerie Fred Jahn, München, *Übermalte Radierungen (Overpainted Etchings)*

2002

Kunst-Raum-Akademie, Akademie der Diözese Rottenburg-Stuttgart, *Abgrund und Transzendenz (Abyss and Transcendence)*

Galerie Oberländer, Augsburg

2003

Galerie Fred Jahn, München, *Arbeiten auf Papier (Works on Paper)*

Galerie Brigitte Knyrim, Regensburg, *Bild, Skulptur, Graphik (Pictures, Sculptures, Graphics)*

galerie am kleinen plan, Celle

2004

Galerie Oberländer, Augsburg, *Bilder (Pictures)*

Galerie Marie-José van de Loo, München, *Neue Arbeiten auf Leinwand (New Works on Canvas)*

Galerie Josephski-Neukum, Issing, *Skulptur, Malerei, Zeichnung, Druckgraphik (Sculptures, Paintings, Drawings, Printed Graphic Works)*

2006

DIE GALERIE, Frankfurt am Main, *Bilder 1970–2006 / Arbeiten auf Papier (Pictures 1970–2006 / Works on Paper)*

2007

Ketterer Kunst, Berlin, *Franz Hitzler bei Ketterer (Franz Hitzler at Ketterer)*

Verein für Original-Radierung München e.V., *Radierungen und Holzschnitte (Etchings and Woodcuts)*

Galerie Donau-Einkaufszentrum, Regensburg, *Retrospektive I Franz Hitzler – Arbeiten auf Papier + Objekte (Retrospective I Franz Hitzler – Works on Paper and Objects)*

Städtische Galerie Regensburg, *Retrospektive II Franz Hitzler – Bild + Montage (Retrospective II Franz Hitzler – Pictures and Montages)*

Galerie Brigitte Knyrim, Regensburg, *Franz Hitzler – Das kleine Format (Franz Hitzler – The Small Format)*

2008

Expressionale Berlin, *Franz Hitzler und Bernd Zimmer*

Galerie Josephski-Neukum, Issing *Malerei, Objekte, Graphik (Painting, Objects, Graphic Works)*

2009

Galerie Biedermann, München, *Neue Arbeiten und Keramiken (New Works and Ceramics)*

Kunsthalle Schweinfurt, *Franz Hitzler / Farbe, Furcht und Engel (Franz Hitzler / Colour, Fear and Angels)* Bilder und Keramiken (Pictures and ceramics)

2010

Künstlerhaus Markt Oberdorf, *Franz Hitzler / Aus der Glut (Franz Hitzler / Out of the Embers)* Bilder und Keramiken. Retrospektive (Pictures and ceramics. Retrospective)

2011

DG Deutsche Gesellschaft für christliche Kunst e.V., München, *Franz Hitzler / Abgrund und Transzendenz (Franz Hitzler / Abyss and Transcendence)*

Galerie Titus Koch, Schloss Randegg, Gottmadingen, *Franz Hitzler / Bilder, Skulpturen und Keramiken (Franz Hitzler / Pictures, Sculptures and Ceramics)*

2012

Schwäbische Galerie im Volkskunde-museum Oberschönenfeld, *Farbgestalt (Colour Formation)* Malerei und Keramik (Pictures and ceramics)

Edition Jürgen B. Tesch

Cover: *Slit Red / Spalt im Rot* (detail / Detail), see p. / siehe S. 91

Frontispiece / Frontispiz: *Franz Hitzler*
Photo © Jürgen B. Tesch

page / Seite 12: *Franz Hitzler*
Photo © stefan moses

page / Seite 124: *Franz Hitzler*
Photo © DIE GALERIE, Frankfurt

Prestel Verlag, Munich

A member of Verlagsgruppe
Random House GmbH
Prestel Verlag
Neumarkter Strasse 28
81673 Munich
Tel. +49 (0)89 4136-0
Fax +49 (0)89 4136-2335

www.prestel.de

Prestel Publishing Ltd.
4 Bloomsbury Place
London WC1A 2QA
Tel. +44 (0)20 7323-5004
Fax +44 (0)20 7636-8004

Prestel Publishing
900 Broadway, Suite 603
New York, NY 10003
Tel. +1 (212) 995-2720
Fax +1 (212) 995-2733

www.prestel.com

Prestel books are available worldwide. Please contact your nearest bookseller or one of the above addresses for information concerning your local distributor.

Die Deutsche Nationalbibliothek verzeichnet diese Publikation in der Deutschen Nationalbibliografie; detaillierte bibliografische Daten sind im Internet über http://www.dnb.de abrufbar.

The Deutsche Bibliothek holds a record of this publication in the Deutsche Nationalbibliografie; detailed bibliographical data can be found under: http://www.dnb.de

The Library of Congress Cataloguing-in-Publication data is available.

British Library Cataloguing-in-Publication Data: a catalogue record for this book is available from the British Library.

Editorial direction / Projektleitung:
Gabriele Ebbecke

Assistance / Assistenz:
Eva Dotterweich

Copy-editing / Lektorat:
Sophie Reinhardt (German / deutsch),
Danko Szabó (English / englisch)

Translation from the German /
Übersetzung aus dem Deutschen:
Jane Michael

Design and / und layout:
WIGEL, Munich

Production / Herstellung:
Andrea Cobré

Origination / Repro:
Reproline Genceller

Printing and binding / Druck und Bindung:

Weber-Offset, München

Printed in Germany

ISBN 978-3-7913-5279-4

FSC
www.fsc.org
MIX
Aus verantwortungsvollen Quellen
FSC® C015562

The FSC-certified paper Hello Fat matt was supplied by Deutsche Papier

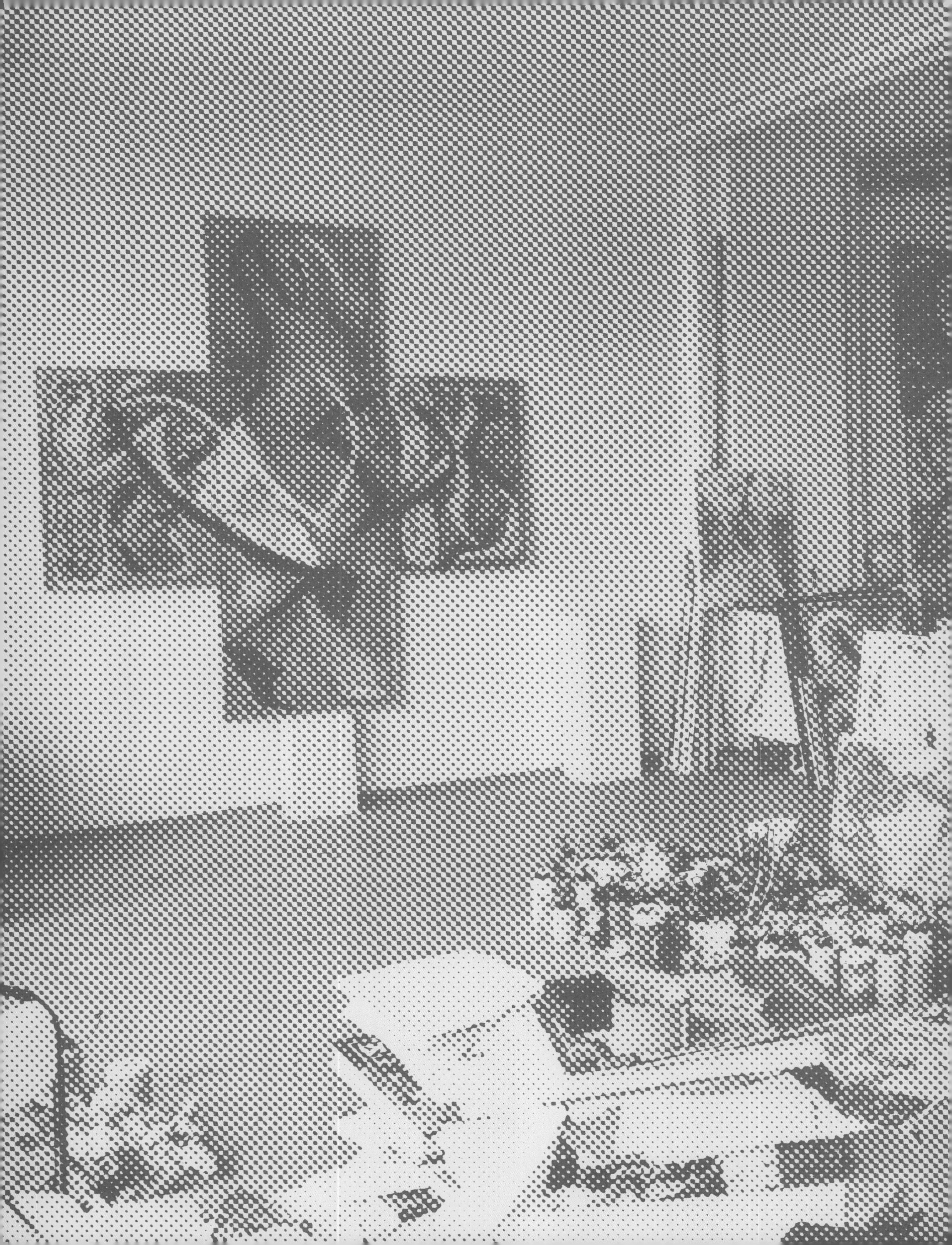